By GORE VIDAL

Novels

WILLIWAW

IN A YELLOW WOOD

THE CITY AND THE PILLAR

THE SEASON OF COMFORT

A SEARCH FOR THE KING

DARK GREEN, BRIGHT RED

THE JUDGMENT OF PARIS

MESSIAH

Plays

VISIT TO A SMALL PLANET *and Other Television Plays*

VISIT TO A SMALL PLANET

THE BEST MAN

Short Stories

A THIRSTY EVIL

THE BEST MAN

The Best Man

A PLAY ABOUT POLITICS

by GORE VIDAL

Little, Brown and Company · BOSTON · TORONTO

LIBRARY OF CONGRESS CATALOG CARD NO. 60-13970

FIRST EDITION

Photographs by courtesy of Abner D. Klipstein

The foreword to this play was published in *Theatre Arts* magazine, July,
1960.

*Published simultaneously in Canada
by Little, Brown & Company (Canada) Limited*

PRINTED IN THE UNITED STATES OF AMERICA

For Roger L. Stevens

The first performance of *The Best Man* in New York City was given on March 31, 1960, at the Morosco Theatre. It was produced by The Playwrights Company, and directed by Joseph Anthony. The setting and lighting were by Jo Mielziner; the costumes were by Theonie V. Aldredge and of course Lyn Austin Associate produced. The cast was as follows:

WILLIAM RUSSELL	Melvyn Douglas
ART HOCKSTADER	Lee Tracy
SENATOR JOE CANTWELL	Frank Lovejoy
ALICE RUSSELL	Leora Dana
MABEL CANTWELL	Kathleen Maguire
MRS. GAMADGE	Ruth McDevitt
DON BLADES	Joseph Sullivan
DICK JENSEN	Karl Weber
SHELDON MARCUS	Graham Jarvis
SENATOR CARLIN	Gordon B. Clarke
DR. ARTINIAN	Hugh Franklin

REPORTER 1: Howard Fischer; REPORTER 2: Tony Bickley; REPORTER 3: Barbara Berjer; REPORTER 4: Tom McDermott. DELEGATES, OTHER REPORTERS: John Dorrin, Mitchell Erickson, Ruth Tobin.

Notes on *The Best Man*

by GORE VIDAL

FOR SOME REASON when it is ninety in the shade and the Hudson River has gone dull-gray and I cross a certain bit of lawn contained by river wall mysteriously, a train of association is set off: I brood on Henry James. I fret about Strether. I deplore the Princess and her treatment of Hyacinth, and (though ripeness is all and the rest is the madness of art) I wonder if, really, I am taken with James's way. Is he too neat? Too artificial? Too classical? Too much devoted to balance? Item: *The Tragic Muse*. Each of four characters begins at the farthest extremity of an X; they cross; each ends in an opposite position. One wonders, does a living pulse beat? Or is it only a metronome?

One day last July, the temperature went to ninety; the river turned a sullen gray; I crossed the brown lawn and started, irritably, to rethink *The Tragic Muse*. No, I did not like the method, I decided. It was all a trick, an easy parlor game. As if one were, in contemporary terms, to take . . . just, for example . . . a man of exemplary private life, yet monstrous public life, and contrast him to a man of "immoral" private life and exemplary public life. That was just the sort of thing James would take on. How he would enjoy mechanically turning the screw upon each character. For sake of argument, make the two men politicians, perhaps fighting one another for the Presidency. Then demonstrate how, in our confused age, morality means, simply, sex found out. To most Americans, cheating, character assassination, hypocrisy, self-seeking are taken quite for granted as the way things are, not pleasant perhaps but: son, you've got to look after number one because there's a lot of competition and . . . By the time I got back to the house to escape the sun and *The Tragic Muse* revisited, I had the characters for *The Best Man*. One very perceptive (if not very flattering) critic recently compared me to Sardou, remarking how I displayed the same dramatic artifice, the well-madeness, the somewhat mechanical balance . . . the critic was right in his intuition, because who did study Sardou devoutly? Disastrously? Not I, but Henry James.

I went off to Provincetown at the end of August. I never had visited the Cape before, knew no one, recalled only that Tennessee Williams once told me it was a good place to work; in fact, he composed *A Streetcar Named Desire* in Provincetown. For once, however, I did not write. I thought. I had the general line of the play clear in my head. Narrative time would be concentrated to the three days preceding a presidential convention. I planned short scenes, alternating between the candidate-suites in a Philadelphia hotel. Yet I had still to make up my mind about the two important issues on which the plot would turn. What in William Russell's past could the opportunist Senator Cantwell use at the last minute which might effectively end his candidacy? And what might Russell find in Cantwell's private life which would, first, stop Cantwell and, second, and morally more important, revolt Russell in the doing?

It was Richard Rovere who gave me the answer to the first: intimations of mental instability. It was a valuable suggestion. The *Zeitgeist* is full now of the buzz of psychoanalysis; everyone's mind is cluttered with at least a few misunderstood clinical phrases and conceptions. If William Russell had once had a nervous breakdown, and Senator Cantwell were to get his hands on Russell's case history and threaten to reveal the contents to the delegates at the convention, it was unlikely Russell could survive

politically. A presidential candidate can have many faults, but
even a hint of mental instability is disqualifying. The second
problem I solved reluctantly. What could be brought up about
Senator Cantwell? I wanted something ambiguous: it might or it
might not be true but, true or not, Russell must resent having to
reveal it, even to save himself. This was limiting. If Cantwell had
stolen money, got a girl pregnant, run away in battle, taken dope,
been a Communist or a member of the Ku Klux Klan, Russell
might be reluctant to bring the matter up, but he would certainly
not hesitate to save himself, especially if he were convinced the
charges were true. Homosexuality was about the only thing left
(no, I have not read *Advise and Consent*). It was a charge which,
true or not, Russell would detest exploiting. It was also an ironic
charge to bring against Cantwell, whose marriage was deliberately made in that heaven where Miss Rose Franken's Claudia
and David were created. Once these two matters were decided,
I was able to write the play in three weeks.

The production went smoothly. I have never been involved in
any dramatic venture in which there was not at least one actor
everyone wished at the end had not been hired. *The Best Man*
company is unique for me: all the actors are very fine and I have
no regrets, only admiration. I found Joseph Anthony an ideal director, particularly complementary to my somewhat dry style.
Anthony has an extraordinary gift for opening up emotional rela-
tionships, for finding small but revelatory character points which
I, intent on the argument, usually miss. I confess, somewhat
sheepishly, that I can find no one to accuse of destroying my
beautiful play, if only because I do not write beautiful plays. I
use the theater as a place to criticize society, to satirize folly,
to question presuppositions. Kenneth Tynan has remarked that I
am not "adventurous" and only at my best as a destructive sat-
irist, but who is not? It is infinitely harder to ask questions in
such a way that the audience is led not to the answers (the

province of the demagogue) but to new perceptions. No writer's conclusions are ever of much interest if only because wisdom, when concentrated, is proverbial. Shaw's conclusions about the Life Force (appropriated from Bergson) are not very helpful, but his method of questioning and burlesquing is his art, and at his best he teases his audiences into asking the right questions. I can think of no other reason to write plays, though other writers have other incentives, equally useful.

I should also mention that Roger L. Stevens showed considerable courage in producing *The Best Man,* shutting his ears to the wounded cries of those distinguished politicians with whom he is associated as a money-raiser for the Democratic Party. To a man they were opposed to the production — I suppose because politicians, like magicians and safe-crackers, do not enjoy being explicated.

ACT ONE

ACT ONE

Scene One

*A hotel suite in Philadelphia . . . perhaps July 1960.
From stage right to left: a bedroom with twin beds, a connecting hall, and a living room. There is a door from living
room to hall and one from bedroom to hall. At stage right,
a door to the bathroom. At stage left, a door to the office
part of the suite, from which can be heard telephones ring-
ing and the buzz of talk.*

*Dominating the living room, stage left, is a television set.
There is also a bar upstage and of course the usual number
of chairs and sofas. The décor is early Conrad Hilton. On
the wall, a poster proclaims* WILLIAM RUSSELL FOR PRESIDENT.
*The candidate, according to his portrait, is a strong, youth-
ful-looking man of fifty. There are also various placards
around the room, propped against walls and furniture:*
HUSTLE WITH RUSSELL . . . , A GREAT GOVERNOR, A GREAT SEC-
RETARY OF STATE, AND THE NEXT PRESIDENT OF THE U.S., *and
similar political sentiments.*

*Since one hotel suite is apt to look very like another, this
same set could be used for the opposition's suite downstairs,
so that when the narrative shifts to the other suite all that
would need changing would be specific props: for instance,
the placards there would itemize the virtues of Senator Joe
Cantwell for President:* YOU'LL DO WELL WITH CANTWELL,
GO WITH JOE, *etc. Fortunately,* The Best Man's *New York*

3

production was designed by Jo Mielziner, a crafty user of twin turntables which made it possible to have two sets which were shifted with great speed. The Cantwell suite resembled the Russell suite in layout, except that everything was reversed: the Cantwell living room was at right and the bedroom at left. The director made an amiable point in furnishing the Russell bedroom with twin beds and the Cantwell bedroom with a double bed.

As the curtain rises, photographers and newsmen set off a great flash of camera bulbs, aimed at WILLIAM *and* ALICE RUSSELL, *who enter from the hall, followed by* REPORTERS, PHOTOGRAPHERS, *a* BELLBOY *and* DICK JENSEN, *Bill Russell's campaign manager.*

JENSEN *is in his late forties: intense, devoted, apprehensive by nature. There is a babble of sound: strident questions — "Any statement?" "What about California?" "The labor bill?" "Just one more, Mr. Secretary," "Red China?" "How many delegates you got?" During this* RUSSELL *tries to be heard; his wife stands rigidly beside him.* ALICE RUSSELL *is in her early forties. She is a handsome, slender, gray-haired lady of the Old American Establishment, not quite as diffident and shy as she appears.*

JENSEN

O.K., boys! O.K. Give him air! One question at a time . . .

REPORTER 1

Mr. Secretary, as of today how many delegates do you have sewed up?

RUSSELL
(*Lightly*)
When it comes to delegates, we neither sow nor do we reap.

REPORTER 1
(*Puzzled*)
What was that again, Mr. Secretary?

RUSSELL
I said . . .

JENSEN
Mr. Russell was making a joke, he means we . . .

REPORTER 2
(*Helpfully*)
He said neither do they sow . . .

REPORTER 3
But what about Ex-President Hockstader? Have you got his endorsement yet?

RUSSELL
In a word . . . no.

REPORTER 3
Do you think you'll get it?

RUSSELL
Ask him. There's a rumor he's in Philadelphia.

REPORTER 4
Yes. He's upstairs. He's going to make a statement tonight. He says it's between you and Senator Cantwell . . .

RUSSELL
So we'll just have to wait until tonight.

REPORTER 1

Mrs. Russell, what do *you* think your husband's chances are?

ALICE

(*Uncertainly*)

Well, I . . . I don't really know. I mean, we have to wait for the convention, don't we?

REPORTER 2

Mr. Secretary, if there's a deadlock between you and Senator Cantwell, whom do you think will be the dark horse candidate?

RUSSELL

Jack Paar. (*Smiles*) I'm sorry, but I'm not about to build up a dark horse when I am doing my best to look like the light horse.

REPORTER 2

Sir, what do you think of Governor Merwin's chances?

RUSSELL

John Merwin is a very talented young man. We don't know much about him, of course, but . . .

REPORTER 4

(*Quickly*)

Would you consider Governor Merwin as a running mate?

REPORTER 3

Yes.

RUSSELL

I might. He's one of a number of capable men.

REPORTER 3

Mr. Secretary, how did you interpret the Gallup poll this morning?

RUSSELL

I didn't interpret it because I didn't see it.

REPORTER 4

Senator Cantwell's picked up two per cent from you since last week . . .

JENSEN

(*Overlapping*)

But we're still leading by nine per cent in the country with . . .

RUSSELL

But you *can* say I don't believe in polls . . .

JENSEN

(*Nervously*)

What the Secretary means is . . .

RUSSELL

(*Firmly*)

I don't believe in polls. Accurate or not. And if I may bore you with one of my little sermons: life is not a popularity contest; neither is politics. The important thing for any government is educating the people about issues, *not* following the ups and downs of popular opinion.

REPORTER 3

(*In for the kill*)

Does that mean you don't respect popular opinion? Do you think a President ought to ignore what the people want?

7

RUSSELL
(*Serenely*)
If the people want the wrong thing, if the people don't understand an issue, if they've been misled by the press (*Politely*) —
by *some* of the press — then I think a President should ignore
their opinion and try to convince them that his way is the right
way.

REPORTER 2
Do you think the people mistrust intellectuals in politics?

RUSSELL
(*Smiles*)
I'm glad you asked that question. Bertrand Russell seems to
think so. He once wrote that the people in a democracy tend to
think they have less to fear from a stupid man than from an in-
telligent one.

REPORTER 1
(*Lost*)
Bertrand . . . ?

RUSSELL
Bertrand Russell.

REPORTER 1
(*Slow, false dawning*)
Oh, the same name . . .

RUSSELL
(*Amused*)
Yes. But no relative, unfortunately.

REPORTER 3
(*The taste of blood*)
Wasn't Bertrand Russell *fired* from City College of New York?

RUSSELL
(*Sadly*)
Yes, he was fired. But only for moral turpitude . . . *not* for incompetence as a philosopher.

REPORTER 4
What image do you feel Senator Cantwell is projecting at the moment?

RUSSELL
Image? He's behaving himself, if that's what you mean.

REPORTER 4
(*Solemnly*)
But hasn't his *basic* image changed in the last year?

RUSSELL
I'm afraid I don't know much about images. That's a word from advertising where you don't sell the product, you sell the image of the product. And sometimes the image is a fake.

REPORTER 3
(*Slyly*)
But after all, your own image . . .

RUSSELL
Is a poor thing but mine own. Paint me as I am, warts and all!

REPORTER 1
What?

RUSSELL

Oliver Cromwell.

(JENSEN *starts rounding up the press*)

JENSEN

O.K., fellows, we'll have a statement for you in about an hour. Headquarters are through there. The mimeograph machine has been repaired and . . .

RUSSELL

And wisdom flows by the yard.

(JENSEN *herds the* REPORTER *off stage left. All except* REPORTER 3. *She has followed* ALICE *into the bedroom.* RUSSELL *says good-by to the* REPORTERS *at the door*)

REPORTER 1
(*Urgently*)

Mr. Secretary . . .

(*A flood of last-minute questions and photographers shouting: "Just one more"*)

RUSSELL
(*Apologetically*)

I have a feeling Dick Jensen would like the candidate to stop talking. I'll see you all later, after the delegations. Until then, as Senator Cantwell would say, may the best man win!

(*The* REPORTERS *and* JENSEN *are gone.* RUSSELL *is relieved until he hears the cold-edged voice of* REPORTER 3 *in the bedroom*)

REPORTER 3

How do you like Philadelphia, Mrs. Russell?

10

ALICE

Well, I just got here . . . I used to visit here as a girl.
(RUSSELL *comes to the rescue. He propels* REPORTER 3 *to the door at stage left*)

RUSSELL

Please, *please*. Wait till we unpack.

REPORTER 3

Do you drink the tap water?

RUSSELL

I have no intention of losing Pennsylvania by admitting that I boil the local water.
(REPORTER 3 *departs with an unamused grimace.* RUSSELL *shudders.* JENSEN *returns*)

JENSEN
(*Groans*)

Bertrand Russell at a press conference.

RUSSELL
(*Placating*)

All right, Dick, all right, no more jokes. From now on we project blandness. A candidate should not mean but be. And no matter *what* happens, I shall smile: serenely, fatuously, ineluctably.
(RUSSELL, *smiling, hat in hand, marches, waving and beaming, to the bedroom*)

RUSSELL
(*Intoning*)

Floods destroy the Middle West, and the candidate smiles.

11

Half the world is starving, and the candidate smiles. War is declared, and the candidate smiles. Is there anything more indecent than the human face when it smiles?

(ALICE *takes the hat. He returns to the connecting hall and looks into the mirror*)

RUSSELL

All these predatory teeth, reminding us of our animal descent.

JENSEN

Steady. No mention of Darwin. Evolution is out of bounds. Before the Garden of Eden was the Word. And *stop* looking in the mirror.

RUSSELL

I never pass a mirror I don't look in it. I wonder why?

(ALICE *has gone to hang a coat in the wall closet. En route, she answers him*)

ALICE
(*Briskly*)

Vanity.

(ALICE *returns to her unpacking in the bedroom*)

RUSSELL
(*Thoughtfully*)

I look to remind myself I really exist. One needs constant proofs.

ALICE

I better use the bathroom while I've got a chance.

RUSSELL
(*Genuine concern*)
Alice, *don't* drink the *water!*
(*The telephone in the living room rings*)

JENSEN
(*Answers it*)
Who? Oh, Mrs. Gamadge, good to hear your voice . . . ! Yes, ma'am. Well, he's got the Texas delegation coming in about twenty minutes, but (*Looks to* RUSSELL *for guidance.* RUSSELL *nods*) if you come over right now . . . Oh, good, you're in the hotel . . . fine. We'll see you then. (*Puts down receiver*) Our national committee woman.

RUSSELL
The only known link between the N.A.A.C.P. and the Ku Klux Klan. How does she do it? How? How?
(RUSSELL *is studying the carpet as he paces oddly downstage*)

JENSEN
(*Curiously*)
Bill . . . may I ask a very personal question?

RUSSELL
Personal? There is no other kind between us . . .

JENSEN
What the hell are you doing when you start that hopscotch thing up and down the floor?

RUSSELL
As we say at press conferences, I'm glad you asked that question. I am . . . oh, damn! (*He steps back suddenly*) The ancient

13

Romans used to examine the entrails of animals in order to learn the future. I am told on very good authority that my rival, Senator Cantwell, goes to an astrologist in Kalorama Road, Washington, for guidance. I, lacking all superstition, study the future in multiples of threes. Put simply — and we are nothing if not experts at putting things simply, are we? — I find a carpet with workable pattern. This one's perfect. Now if I step on a leaf — see? — before I have completed three full steps *between* leaves, I will *not* get what I want. If, however, I can take three paces *without* touching that leaf, I will get what I want. I may say, I never cheat. (*Scowls*) Hell! However, I can on occasion go for the best two out of three. I also make bets with myself. For instance, if the man I'm talking to does not answer me within the count of three, I get what I want. (*He finishes his walk just short of where* JENSEN *is seated at stage left*) Ah, victory! I hope I've answered your question lucidly?

JENSEN

Yes, you have. But let's keep it *our* secret. (*A* WOMAN AID *enters with a stack of newspapers from left*) My own vice is the daily horoscope. (AID *goes*) So what did you win?

RUSSELL

The nomination. And on the first ballot, too! (*He sits on downstage sofa*) My God, I'm keyed up! I feel like I'm going to jump out of my skin. I can't sit still . . .
(JENSEN *crosses to him*)

JENSEN

Well, you won't do much sitting still between now and Wednesday. Here's today's schedule. Most of the delegations will come to us. (*Shows* RUSSELL *paper*) See? It's a tight schedule, starting with Texas at 11:15, then . . .

14

RUSSELL

(*Unable to attend*)

We're getting so close . . . so close! And what's going to happen?

JENSEN

You! We've got the delegates. It's yours on the first ballot. *If you get Ex-President Hockstader's endorsement . . .*

(*The door buzzer in the connecting hall sounds. There is a noise of voices from the outside corridor*)

RUSSELL AND JENSEN

(*In unison*)

Mrs. Gamadge!

(*They both cross to the hall door.* JENSEN *opens it.* MRS. GAMADGE, *small, plump, elderly, sails into view, surrounded by* NEWSMEN *and* PHOTOGRAPHERS. *She is serene in the knowledge that she is the Voice of the American Woman, by default. Her manner is an odd mixture of coziness and steeliness*)

MRS. GAMADGE

(*Beams*)

Mr. Secretary . . .

(MRS. GAMADGE *seizes* RUSSELL *for a picture. They pose, her left arm around him, her right arm raised in salute. Then* JENSEN *ushers out the press*)

RUSSELL

(*Sudden energy*)

Mrs. Gamadge, it's wonderful to see you! Come on in. Sit down. Have a drink. You know Dick Jensen, don't you? My campaign manager.

15

(MRS. GAMADGE *shakes* JENSEN's *hand as she crosses to a sofa*)

MRS. GAMADGE

Such a lovely hotel for a convention. I always say the hotel you're at makes all the difference at a convention. Does Mrs. Russell like your suite?

RUSSELL

Practically a home away from home.

MRS. GAMADGE
(*Narrowly*)

She *is* here with you, isn't she?
(RUSSELL *pulls out a chair for her*)

RUSSELL

Yes. This is the good chair.

MRS. GAMADGE

I'll sit *here,* thank you.
(MRS. GAMADGE *unfurls on the sofa*)

JENSEN

I must say, I'm glad to meet you at last, Mrs. Gamadge.

MRS. GAMADGE

And I'm glad to get a chance to see you, Mr. Jensen. I love eggheads in politics.

JENSEN
(*Taken aback*)

Oh, well . . .

16

RUSSELL
(*Quickly*)
What can I get you to drink?

MRS. GAMADGE
I don't drink, Mr. Secretary. A Coke or a glass of soda, maybe. Anything. (*Turns to* JENSEN, *sweetly*) Professors like you give such a tone to these conventions. No, I really mean it. Of course a lot of the women don't like them but I do. Though of course I didn't like the New Deal.
(RUSSELL *gives her a glass*)

RUSSELL
Here's your soda . . .
(*She takes it with a nice smile*)

MRS. GAMADGE
A great many of the women are suspicious of you professors, Mr. Jensen. . . . You don't mind my speaking like this?

JENSEN
Certainly not, Mrs. Gamadge. After all, talking to you is like . . . well, like talking to the average American housewife. (JENSEN *is aware* MRS. GAMADGE *has frozen on "average." He stammers*) I mean *you're* not average but you speak for them . . .

MRS. GAMADGE
Very nicely put, Mr. Jensen. (*To* RUSSELL) I don't know why everyone says he's so conceited.

RUSSELL
Dick? Stuck up? Why, he's the spirit of humility . . . an old

17

shoe, in fact! As for being intellectual, he can hardly get through the Greek Anthology without a trot.

MRS. GAMADGE
(*Nods*)

Yes. (*To business*) You see, the women like a regular kind of man, like General Eisenhower. Now he really appeals to the women. That nice smile. He has such a way with him . . . he inspires confidence because he doesn't seem like anything but *just folks*. You could imagine him washing up after dinner, listening to his wife's view on important matters.

RUSSELL
(*Quietly*)

Yes, indeed you can.

MRS. GAMADGE

Nothing pushy or aggressive or all those things we women don't like in our men. He's just grand! Now, Mr. Secretary, there is no doubt in anybody's mind you are going to get the nomination on the first ballot . . .

RUSSELL

There is doubt in *my* mind . . .

MRS. GAMADGE
(*No time for diversion*)

Yes . . . yes . . . yes . . . now let's face facts a minute. You don't mind if I talk turkey?

RUSSELL

No. By all means . . . turkey.

18

MRS. GAMADGE

You are not the ideal candidate for the women. You know that, I suppose.

RUSSELL

Well, what . . . what women do you have in mind?

MRS. GAMADGE
(*Coldly*)
The women don't like your trying to be funny all the time.

RUSSELL

No, no. It is a flaw, I agree.

MRS. GAMADGE

The women are *very* suspicious of a man who doesn't take things seriously. So just don't try to be smart-aleck and talk over their heads. I hope you don't mind my talking like this but there isn't much time.

RUSSELL

I am certainly grateful for your . . . candor.
(MRS. GAMADGE *rises and circles with empty glass toward the bar*)

MRS. GAMADGE

Now we want to see more of your wife. A lot more.

RUSSELL
(RUSSELL *sits stage left*)
She was sick, you know, during the primaries . . .

19

MRS. GAMADGE

And your two fine sons. They're very attractive and that was a nice spread of them in *Life*, at the barbecue. Very, very nice. We'll want more of that. But most important, your wife should be at your side at all times. She must *seem* to be advising you. The women must feel that there is a woman behind you (MRS. GAMADGE *has maneuvered herself into position behind* RUSSELL's *chair*), as there has been a woman behind every great man since the world began!

(RUSSELL, *aware of* MRS. GAMADGE's *presence, rises and crosses to* JENSEN *at right*)

RUSSELL

Alice plans to campaign with me, if . . .

MRS. GAMADGE

She's a tremendous asset. I don't need to tell you. The women like the way she doesn't wear make-up and looks like a lady, and seems shy . . .

RUSSELL

She is shy.

MRS. GAMADGE

She doesn't make the women feel jealous. And that's good. Keep her with you, Mr. Secretary, at all times. It did Adlai Stevenson great harm, not having a wife, and trying to be funny all the time, too. Great harm. (MRS. GAMADGE *returns to sofa and sits down*) Now I want to ask you a blunt question: what truth is there in the rumor that there has been . . . marital discord between you and Mrs. Russell?

20

RUSSELL
(*Evenly*)

Mrs. Gamadge, my wife is here in Philadelphia. If I am nominated, she will do everything possible to be a helpful candidate's wife . . .

MRS. GAMADGE

Could I see her?

RUSSELL

Of course. (*Crosses to bedroom door*) Alice . . . come on out and meet Mrs. Gamadge.

(ALICE *signals* RUSSELL *to wait while she arranges her blouse*)

MRS. GAMADGE
(*To* JENSEN)

Now Mabel Cantwell is *such* a nice woman. Really one of the girls. You feel like you've known her all your life. Last time I was in Washington, Mabel gave this lovely dessert luncheon for me with four tables of canasta . . .

(*Somewhat nervously*, ALICE *enters and starts to cross to* MRS. GAMADGE, *who has risen and, to her alarm, started backing away with a speculative look, taking in everything*)

ALICE

How very nice to see you . . .

MRS. GAMADGE
(*Slowly, deliberately*)

You . . . couldn't . . . look . . . better! I mean it! I like the whole thing . . . especially the naturally gray hair, that is *such* an important point with the women. Of course Mabel Cantwell

21

dyes her hair, but she gets away with it because she does such a bad job the women feel sorry for her.

(*A* WOMAN AID *enters from left. She gives* JENSEN *a note and goes.* JENSEN *shows the note to* RUSSELL. MRS. GAMADGE *observes this byplay*)

MRS. GAMADGE

Oh, I know you have a million things to do! Anyway, I just want you to know that I'm for you, Mr. Secretary, and I'm sure you and Mrs. Russell are a winning team. (*To* ALICE, *cozily*) When you're the First Lady just remember this: don't do too much . . . like Mrs. Roosevelt. The women didn't like that. On the other hand, don't do too little . . . like Mrs. Eisenhower. The women don't like that either. All in all, Grace Coolidge was really the best, bless her heart. My husband had such a crush on her . . .

JENSEN

How *is* Mr. Gamadge?
(RUSSELL *signals belatedly but the gaffe is made*)

MRS. GAMADGE
(*Quietly*)

Mr. Gamadge passed on in 1956. He was stricken during the New Hampshire primaries.

JENSEN

Oh, I didn't know that. I'm sorry . . .

MRS. GAMADGE

So am I. He was a fine man, though he didn't like politics. He suffered his terminal thrombosis while I was in Wisconsin, that same year. (*Hearty handclasp*) Bill, *go to it!* The women are in your corner!

RUSSELL

You don't know how much that means to me . . . Sue-Ellen.

MRS. GAMADGE

(*To* ALICE, *warmly*)

Us girls will have a get-together real soon. And that's a promise.

ALICE

I do hope so, Mrs. Gamadge.

MRS. GAMADGE

(*At the door, the knife*)

Oh, by the way! A little bird tells me Joe Cantwell has a surprise for you.

RUSSELL

A surprise?

MRS. GAMADGE

Uh-huh. He's going to smear you with something . . . so they say.

RUSSELL

(*Startled*)

Smear me?

MRS. GAMADGE

(*Gaily*)

But here I am telling you what you already know. I'm sure you can handle it. 'By, Bill. 'By, Dick!

(*In a burst of sound from the newsmen in the corridor,* MRS. GAMADGE *goes*)

ALICE

Smear you, Bill? With what?

RUSSELL
(*Frowns*)

I don't know.

(JENSEN *waves note*)

JENSEN

Well, Alice, word has come from on high. We're about to have a visit from our distinguished Ex-President.

ALICE

I must say he's one of the ones I like . . . except when he tells those long stories.

RUSSELL

Which will it be? The kiss . . . or the knife.

JENSEN

How can you miss? Like the rest of us he loves a winner.

ALICE

And he does like *you*, Bill.

RUSSELL

I don't know. He's a funny old bird.

(WOMAN AID *appears in doorway left*)

JENSEN

Yes?

AID

The "Volunteer Women for Russell" are on the mezzanine. They want to know if they can see Mrs. Russell.

24

RUSSELL

Are you up to it?

ALICE

Of course I am. Tell them I'll join them in a few minutes.
(ALICE *goes into bedroom to get ready.* WOMAN *gives several sheets to* JENSEN)

AID

Copies of the Secretary's speech for tonight.

JENSEN

I'll check them now.
(AID *goes, left*)

RUSSELL
(*Indicates speech*)
You might let me look at it, too. I'd like to know what I'm saying.

JENSEN

Come off it, your speech writers . . .
(RUSSELL *takes the speech and glances through it*)

RUSSELL

. . . are the best money can buy. They have written speeches for Eisenhower, Truman, Dewey, Hockstader, Roosevelt, Hoover and Harold Stassen. Which proves they are men of overpowering conviction.

JENSEN

Do you want to write four speeches a day on top of everything else?

RUSSELL

Of course I want to. But I can't. There isn't time. But it's a shameful business, speech by committee . . .

JENSEN

Not to mention *President* by committee.
(RUSSELL *hands back the speech*)

RUSSELL

Please tell the writers *again* that the word "alternative" is always singular. There is only *one* alternative per situation.

JENSEN

I will denounce them as anti-semanticists . . .
(JENSEN *goes off left.* RUSSELL, *thoughtfully, goes into bedroom*)

RUSSELL

Only one alternative per situation . . . unfortunately. That's grammar.

ALICE

(*Dryly*)
And marriage. . . . Oh, I left my handbag . . .
(ALICE *goes into bathroom.* RUSSELL *starts to unpack a suitcase. She returns*)

RUSSELL

I'm sorry we're . . . in such close quarters.

ALICE

I don't mind. If you don't.

RUSSELL

Odd, after all these years apart. Separate rooms, separate lives.

ALICE

(*Smiles*)

As someone sooner or later says: politics make strange bed-fellows.

RUSSELL

Yes.

ALICE

Certainly there's nothing stranger than the two of us in the same room.

RUSSELL

I don't suppose I'm the first candidate to be in this situation.

ALICE

Bill . . . don't apologize. I said I'd do what I could to help. And I will. Besides, I really want you to be President.

RUSSELL

Why?

ALICE

I don't know. Perhaps I'm unexpectedly ambitious. Perhaps I want to be First Lady. Or perhaps I look forward to seeing you occasionally. (*Quickly*) Don't look alarmed! Only in line of duty. You know, an unexpected meeting in the East Room, an ambiguous encounter in the Lincoln Bedroom . . .

27

RUSSELL
(Amused)

Alice . . .

ALICE

Yesterday, a woman from the press wanted to know what changes I would make when we moved into the White House. I said nothing of a *structural* nature would be changed . . . Will it?

RUSSELL
(Awkwardly)

You know . . . I *do* like the idea of the two of us back together again.

ALICE
(Suddenly sharp)

Bill, I am not a delegation from the Legion of Decency. You don't have to charm me.

(ALICE goes to hall, hangs up a blouse)

RUSSELL

I wasn't trying to. I mean it. I know it's tough . . .

ALICE

Tough? *(Returns to bedroom)* Only for you. You're the one who has a problem. How to get girls into the White House. Or will you have a special place on K Street where the President, in disguise of course, can meet new . . . people.

(RUSSELL scowls and goes into bathroom with his shaving gear)

RUSSELL

(*From the bathroom*)

Why do you say things like that?

ALICE

Obviously because I'm frustrated. Isn't that the usual excuse women give? And isn't that the usual reason?

(RUSSELL *returns to the bedroom, and his unpacking*)

RUSSELL

When the desire to make love to someone goes, it goes and nothing on earth can bring it back. Between us, it went.

ALICE

For you.

RUSSELL

I suppose what I wanted in marriage was a friend.

ALICE

And instead you got a very conventional girl who wanted a husband, who wanted . . . No. I will *not* put on that record again. I don't know why but we never manage to say anything new when we get onto the subject of my inadequacy and your . . . what shall we call it this time? Athleticism? Since according to the ground rules of our marriage we may call it anything except plain old-fashioned promiscuity.

RUSSELL

Look, if you'd rather not be with me, and have to go through with this . . . this gloomy farce, then don't. Quit! Right now.

ALICE

Quit? Certainly not. I like circuses. Besides, I'm good for you, isn't that what Dr. Artinian said? After your breakdown? You are the link, he said, between father and sons, between William Russell and the world.

RUSSELL

Dr. Artinian was right.

ALICE

But I wonder what I would have done that summer at Watch Hill, when we first met at the club, if someone had said: "The handsome young man you've just fallen in love with will always need you . . . *as a link.*" I think if I had known then what I know now I would have slashed my wrists in front of the buffet table and beautifully bled to death between the chicken salad and the lobster Newburgh.

RUSSELL
(*Smiles*)

Luckily, you are not given to melodrama.
(*Both go into living room*)

ALICE

Not yet anyway. But you are very nearly a great man and I suppose I can endure anything because of that. . . . So here we are.

RUSSELL

Somewhat past our youth . . . and friends?

ALICE

It would be nice if we were, wouldn't it? Do I look all right for the "Volunteer Women for Russell"?

RUSSELL

You do.

ALICE
(Dryly)

I ought to. I am a founding member of that considerable body.
(ART HOCKSTADER, *a former President, in his late seventies but alert despite his years, enters from the bathroom door at right. He crosses warily to the connecting hall, where he sees* ALICE, *who is about to go*)

HOCKSTADER

Hi, honey . . .
(ALICE *is startled*)

ALICE

Oh! Mr. President!

HOCKSTADER

You look mighty pretty, Miss Alice . . . as usual!
(HOCKSTADER's *accent is rural American*)

RUSSELL
(Joining them)

Mr. President!

HOCKSTADER

Just plain Art Hockstader to you . . .

ALICE

Where did you come from?

31

THE BEST MAN

HOCKSTADER

(*Indicates right*)

Through the privy. There's a door into the next suite. I sneaked through.

ALICE

You look wonderful, after your operation!

HOCKSTADER

Ought to. Nothin but a hernia from bouncin my grandson too hard.

RUSSELL

What can I get you to drink? No, no, don't tell me . . . bourbon and branch water.

(RUSSELL *goes to the living-room bar*)

HOCKSTADER

With which I shall strike a blow for liberty. (*To the departing* ALICE) Don't let anyone know I'm here. (ALICE *nods and goes*) Well, son, how do you like politics?

RUSSELL

I like it so much I'm beginning to worry.

HOCKSTADER

Awful, ain't it? Worse than gamblin, I sometimes think. Me, I was hooked when I was no more than this high (*Indicates a child*), and a certain fourflusher named William Jennings Bryan came to town. His last campaign, I guess. . . . Well, they shot the works: torchlight parade, picnic, the works! Then finally up there on the back of an old dray, out in a field, this fellow gets up and you never heard such hollerin from a crowd. Big man he

32

was or so he looked to me, about nine foot tall with hair sweeping over his collar and that square red face of his, and when he spoke I tell you it was like thunder on a summer evenin and everythin was still, listenin. I used to know that speech by heart, it was the famous one. (*Imitates a fustian political voice*) "You shall not press down upon the brow of labor this crown of thorns. You shall not crucify mankind upon a cross of gold!"

RUSSELL

Hurray!

(RUSSELL *gives* HOCKSTADER *his drink*)

HOCKSTADER

You betcha! Anyway, it was then and there that a certain farm boy named Art Hockstader said: I am goin to be a politician and get the folks riled up and eat plenty of barbecue and fried chicken at picnics and have all the pretty girls a-hangin on my every word.

RUSSELL

(*Carefully*)

Your endorsement, Art, is a very important thing for anybody who wants to be nominated.

HOCKSTADER

I know it is. (*Smiles*) So, indulge an old duffer! After all, gettin you fellows to listen to my stories and squirm a bit, waitin to see who I'm goin to put my money on, I tell you it's about the only pleasure I got left.

RUSSELL

I'm squirming.

HOCKSTADER
(*Gentle sadism*)
Bill, I have a fatherly feeling about you . . .

RUSSELL
And I have . . .

HOCKSTADER
(*Continues through him*)
Even though I have certain doubts about you.

RUSSELL
Doubts?

HOCKSTADER
(*Nods*)
I'm kind of responsible for your career. You were *my* Secretary of State, and you were a swell one . . . but as you know the people don't give a damn about Secretaries of State. They think the whole foreign thing's a mess anyway and the man who's got to deal with it . . . well, I'm afraid the plain folks think the Secretary of State by definition is a foreigner.

RUSSELL
(*Ruefully*)
I know. And if he doesn't like it here he better go back where he came from.

HOCKSTADER
Exactly. Of course you were a fine governor before that. Though Rhode Island is hardly what we call a king-makin state. . . . Anyway, it isn't your ability I doubt. Hell, you're ten times as well qualified as I was, and look at me! Possibly one of the greatest statesmen of all time!

RUSSELL

You were pretty good.

HOCKSTADER

I certainly was. (*Dryly*) Though it's practically our secret right now, as there has been no overpowering popular movement to add me to that rock garden at Mt. Rushmore. But that's not for me to worry about. No, my objection to you, I guess, was prejudice. For one thing you're a Fancy Dan from the East. But I am nothin if not a realist. The Age of the Great Hicks to which I belong is over. The people trust you rich boys, figurin since you got a lot of money of your own you won't go stealin theirs. I'm sure those people who like this Rockefeller are really thinkin in the back of their minds if they make him President he might decide to pay off the national debt out of his own pocket! If he would, *I'd* vote for him.

RUSSELL

What do you think of Joe Cantwell?

HOCKSTADER
(*Smiles*)

That's a leading question.

RUSSELL

Well, I *am* proposing myself as a leader.

HOCKSTADER

O.K., I'll follow. Joe Cantwell is nothin but ambition. Just plain naked ambition.

RUSSELL

And to get himself elected he will lie . . .

HOCKSTADER
(*Nods*)

Yep.

RUSSELL

He will cheat . . .

HOCKSTADER

Yep.

RUSSELL

He will destroy the reputations of others . . .

HOCKSTADER

Yep.

RUSSELL

Good. So I assume you are endorsing me for the nomination.

HOCKSTADER

Hell, no! Because he's a bastard don't mean he wouldn't be a good candidate. Or even a good President . . .

RUSSELL

Joe Cantwell a good . . . ! You're not serious.

HOCKSTADER

Well, he's got a real sense of how to operate.

RUSSELL

To operate? No. To accommodate! If the people are conservative . . .

HOCKSTADER

He'll be conservative.

RUSSELL

And if they're radical . . .

HOCKSTADER

He'll be radical. Oh, I tell you, son, he is a kind of ring-tailed wonder and don't you underestimate him.

RUSSELL

I don't.

HOCKSTADER

Of course he hasn't got your brains, but then very few of us are as bright as you.

RUSSELL

Now, Art . . .

HOCKSTADER

No, I mean it. You are a superior man of the sort we don't get very often in politics. While Joe's just another of the mediocre boys, like me . . . only smoother of course. A newer model.

RUSSELL

No, he is *not* like you. He'll do anything to win. And that makes him dangerous.

HOCKSTADER

Now I wouldn't go that far. (*The first turn to the screw*) At least he knows his own mind.

37

RUSSELL

And you think I don't know my own mind?

HOCKSTADER

(*Equably*)

Well, son, you got such a good mind that sometimes you're so busy thinkin how complex everything is important problems don't get solved.

RUSSELL

(*Smiles*)

No, I am not that subtle. I am not that undecided. I am not Prince Hamlet.

HOCKSTADER

(*A diversion*)

Hamlet! Lot of fine speeches in that play. Lot of fine speeches in *you*, Bill.

RUSSELL

(*Urgently*)

Art, *don't* support Cantwell!

HOCKSTADER

Now, what makes you think I'm goin to?

RUSSELL

I mean it. And I am not thinking about myself. I'm thinking about the country.

HOCKSTADER

You got to admit, Joe Cantwell ain't afraid to act.

RUSSELL

Neither am I afraid to act.

HOCKSTADER

(*Dreamily*)

Oh? Well, now, I seem to recall how once when you were at a conference with the Russians you were all set to agree to continue nuclear tests, but then when the roof fell in on my administration, I found you had gone and talked yourself up the other side of the street.

RUSSELL

I hesitated only because . . .

HOCKSTADER

I'll say you hesitated. Now you don't catch Joe Cantwell hesitatin. No, sir. He's sharp. He's tough.

RUSSELL

He is not tough. He is expedient and that's a very different thing, and I promise you if Joe were President he'd be the greatest appeaser in history.

HOCKSTADER

I would hardly call him an appeaser . . .

RUSSELL

Suppose the Chinese were to threaten to occupy India and we were faced with the possibility of a world war, the *last* world war. Now that is the kind of thing you and I understand and I think we could handle it without going to war and without losing India. But what would Joe do? He would look at the Gallup poll. And what would the Gallup poll tell him? Well, ask the average

American, do you want to run the risk of being blown up to save India? And he'll say, hell, no! Joe would do the popular thing: to hell with India, and we would be the weaker for it, and that day we're all afraid of would be closer.

(HOCKSTADER *finishes his drink and rises*)

HOCKSTADER

Son, you've been reading too much of that Joe Alsop fellow. Things are never *that* bad! (*Thoughtfully*) Bill, you know it gets mighty lonely in the White House. Worse for me, I guess, than for you. I'd never lived in a big house with a lot of servants, the way you were brought up. But the worst part is, there's nobody you can believe . . . that's the awful thing: everybody's lying to you all day long. . . . Then my wife died . . . (*Sighs*) The wonder is that most of us aren't worse than we are. (*Suddenly*) Bill, do you believe in God?

RUSSELL
(*Startled*)
Do I . . . ? Well, I was confirmed in the Episcopal Church.

HOCKSTADER
Hell, that wasn't what I asked. I'm a Methodist and I'm still askin: do you believe there's a God and a Day of Judgment and a Hereafter?

RUSSELL
No. I believe in us. In man.

HOCKSTADER
(*Nods*)
I've often pretended I thought there was a God, for political purposes.

RUSSELL

(*Smiles*)

So far I haven't told a lie in this campaign. I've never used the word "God" in a speech.

HOCKSTADER

Well, the world's changed since I was politickin. In those days you had to pour God over everything, like ketchup. (*He sits on the bench downstage*) No, I don't believe there's a Hereafter. We pass this way just once. And then . . . nothing. Bill, I am dying.

RUSSELL

(*Stunned*)

What?

HOCKSTADER

That thing about the hernia was just another lie, I'm afraid. (*Dryly*) I hope you don't disapprove. . . . I got the doctors to say the operation was a great success, but it wasn't. I got cancer of the innerds and they tell me I may last just long enough to attend the next Inaugural.

(RUSSELL *rises, crosses to him*)

RUSSELL

Art, I'm . . . ! Look, isn't there . . .

HOCKSTADER

There is nothin they can do, except give me these pills to cut the pain. I tell you, son, I am scared to death. (*Laughs*) That's a phrase for you: "Scared to death" is exactly right. I don't fancy being nothin, just a pinch of dust. No, sir, I don't like that at all.

(RUSSELL *puts his hand on* HOCKSTADER's *shoulder*)

41

RUSSELL

I wish I could say something reassuring, but you wouldn't fall for it anyway.

(HOCKSTADER *shrugs away* RUSSELL's *hand*)

HOCKSTADER

The only good thing I find is that the rest of you sons of bitches are going to join me. There's some consolation I reckon in that. (*Sighs*) Oh, I tell you if there is any point to this universe it sure as hell evades me.

RUSSELL

The whole thing's a tragedy. For all of us. (*Crosses to the sofa*) But there's hope in this: Every act we make sets off a chain of reaction which never ends. And if we are reasonably . . . good, well, there *is* some consolation in that, a kind of immortality.

HOCKSTADER
(*Dryly*)

I suggest you tell yourself that when *you* finally have to face a whole pile of nothin up ahead. (*Rises briskly*) But at the moment I'm alive. And we go into the convention hall day after tomorrow and act like life is all there is . . . which, come to think of it, is true.

(JENSEN *looks in from the office at left*)

JENSEN

The Texas Delegation is here. (*Sees Hockstader*) Oh, Hello, Mr. . . .

(HOCKSTADER *motions to* JENSEN *to say nothing.* JENSEN *nods and shuts the door*)

42

HOCKSTADER

Bill, don't tell anybody what I told you.

RUSSELL

Of course not.

HOCKSTADER

Meanwhile, I am going to keep you in suspense, until tonight at dinner.

RUSSELL

And then?

HOCKSTADER

I will throw my support like a bridal bouquet to the lucky man. (HOCKSTADER *beams; he starts to cross to hall; he pauses*) Oh, these rumors about you and your lady friends . . . won't do you a bit of harm. *But* keep out of trouble. You haven't gone and written any letters like some fellows do?

RUSSELL
(*Smiles*)

No. No letters.

HOCKSTADER

Good boy. She's a nice girl, Alice.

RUSSELL

I think so.

HOCKSTADER
(*Slyly*)
And you never tell a lie, do you? Well, good! Glad to hear it!

(*Grimaces with pain*) Christ, that upper plate of mine pinches! I was going to get a new one but they said it would take a couple of months to make. So I figured I could hold out with what I got.
(*Both men are now at the hall*)

RUSSELL

Art . . .
(*There are several whoops and rebel yells from stage left*)

HOCKSTADER

You go on in there with those crazy Texans. (*Chuckles*) I sure wish I was a fly on that wall, listening to you tell the whole *truth* about what you really think of the depletion of oil resources allowance!

RUSSELL
(*Laughs*)

Get out of here, you old bum . . .
(*Both men are now in the bedroom.* HOCKSTADER *smiles, as he crosses to the bathroom door at right*)

HOCKSTADER

Now is that a respectful way to talk to the end of an era? The last of the Great Hicks as he shuffles off the stage? By way of the privy.
(HOCKSTADER *waves as he exits.* RUSSELL *goes back into the living room.* JENSEN *enters*)

JENSEN
(*Eagerly*)

Well? What did he say?

RUSSELL

He won't let us know till tonight.

JENSEN

He's going to come out for you. I know it!

RUSSELL

(*Slowly*)

No, he's going to support Joe Cantwell.

JENSEN

(*Startled*)

What! Oh, you're out of your mind. Come on, hurry up, the natives of Texas are getting restless. Now remember on the oil issue . . .

RUSSELL

I know. I know. Double talk! (*As he follows* JENSEN *off right*) For those whom we are about to deceive, oh Lord, make us truly compassionate!

CURTAIN

ACT ONE

Scene Two

The Cantwell suite. A few minutes later. MABEL CANT-
WELL, *a blonde, pretty woman of forty in a dresing gown,
lies on a sofa, watching television and drinking a martini.
Around the room, placards and posters implore us to vote
for Senator Joe Cantwell.*

COMMENTATOR'S VOICE
This is John Fox with the news. Well, I guess you all know this
has been some day for Philadelphia, a real old-fashioned convention day, first since 1940. We got some pictures here of the candi-
dates arriving at the Thirtieth Street station. There's the front-
runner, William Russell, with Mrs. Russell . . .

MABEL
(Perfunctorily)
Boo!

COMMENTATOR'S VOICE
Then, just before noon, Senator Joe Cantwell arrived.

MABEL
Yea, team!
(MABEL'S *accent is Southern*)

COMMENTATOR'S VOICE
There he is getting off the train. And there's His Honor again,

46

meeting him. The Senator's with Don Blades, his campaign manager. Oh, and there's *Mrs.* Cantwell.

(MABEL *is suddenly alert. She studies herself carefully on the screen*)

> MABEL
> (*Alarm*)

Oh, my Lord, that hat!

(MABEL *goes into the bedroom, picks up the offending hat and goes into bathroom to try it on. The television set continues to sound*)

> REPORTER'S VOICE

Senator, do you have a statement . . . ? We're here to . . .

> CANTWELL'S VOICE

All I can say is that come Wednesday I only hope that the best man wins . . .

> MABEL
> (*Mechanically from bathroom*)

. . . the best man wins.

(*There is a noise of* REPORTERS *as the hall door opens.* DON BLADES, *a lean gray man, ushers the smiling* JOE CANTWELL *into the living room.* CANTWELL *is in his forties. His manner is warm, plausible. Though under great tension, he suggests ease. He has a tendency not to listen when preoccupied. He poses for one more photograph, arms victoriously raised. Then* BLADES *gets the reporters out.* CANTWELL *relaxes full-length on the sofa*)

> BLADES

That went well, Joe. (*Turns off set*) You better rest before dinner.

CANTWELL

About Hockstader, what did he say when you saw him? What *exactly* did he say?

BLADES
(*For the hundredth time*)
He said he hadn't made up his mind, but he would by tonight.

CANTWELL
(*Calls*)
Mabel, honey! Come on out. It's just Don Blades and me.
(MABEL *appears. She throws herself on him. They embrace warmly*)

CANTWELL
(*Laughing*)
Hey, come on! You better get dressed. We got to go down to dinner in (*Looks at watch*) thirty minutes.

MABEL
I'll be ready . . . don't you worry, baby. Fix yourself a drink, Don.
(BLADES *is at the bar upstage*)

BLADES
Can I get you anything, Mabel?

MABEL
Oh, no, I don't think so. I don't . . . well, maybe just the teeniest martini, to settle my stomach. (*Concern*) Oh, Joe, you look so tired.

CANTWELL
(*Automatically*)
Never felt better.

(CANTWELL *picks up a newspaper and reads, frowning*)

MABEL

Well, I finally got through that women's tea and I've been here watching the TV. We got awful nice coverage, Joe . . . though that new hat of mine is clearly a mistake. It looks like I have no chin, but even with no chin I certainly look better than Alice Russell. My God, she is a chilly-looking woman, just like an English teacher I had back at State College, the spittin image . . . from Boston she was and always wore her hair in this bun with no make-up and of course thought she was the cat's meow . . .

(BLADES *gives her a drink*)

BLADES

Here you go, Mabel.

MABEL

Thank you, Don.

CANTWELL

Hey, Don, that joke of yours looks pretty good.

BLADES

Oh? Which one was that?

CANTWELL

(*Reads*)

"At his press conference yesterday, Senator Cantwell quipped: 'Bill Russell has more solutions than there are problems.'"

(MABEL *tastes the martini. She sighs*)

49

MABEL

Don, the best martinis are made five to one, not five to four.

BLADES

I never could make a mixed drink.

MABEL
(*To* CANTWELL)

All the papers say Hockstader's going to come out for Bill Russell, heaven knows why, with your record in the Senate . . .

CANTWELL
(*Shuts his eyes*)

I am tired. (*Then he sits up, abruptly. He turns to* BLADES) I got to see Hockstader. Right now. Before that dinner.

BLADES

What are you going to tell him?

CANTWELL

Everything. The works. Maybe he won't come out for me afterwards but he'll sure drop Bill Russell.

BLADES
(*Rises*)

O.K. You're the boss.

CANTWELL

Go on up there. He's on the seventh floor. Tell him I've *got* to see him before dinner which is in (*Looks at watch*) twenty-seven minutes.

50

BLADES

Aye, aye, my captain.

(CANTWELL *is on his feet. He turns irritably to* MABEL)

CANTWELL

Mabel, come on, get dressed!

MABEL

I'll be ready, Joe, stop worryin . . . don't get all het up. (*She embraces him*) Why is big Poppa Bear so mean to poor little Momma Bear?

CANTWELL

Baby, I'm sorry. (*He goes into their private baby talk*) Poppa Bear is never mean to his Momma Bear, never ever. (*His own voice*) But, honey, you've *got* to get dressed!

MABEL

O.K., I will . . . I will. Joe, when are you going to spring that . . . that stuff about Bill Russell?

CANTWELL

Tomorrow.

MABEL

The *whole* thing?

CANTWELL

Pow!

(CANTWELL *goes into bedroom, searching for his electric razor*)

MABEL

(*Rapturously*)

And then we are on our way to 1600 Pennsylvania Avenue!

Oh, my, it's thrilling, isn't it? Seems just like yesterday we were skimpin along hardly able to pay the bills to have Gladys's teeth straightened, and now just look at us! Poppa Bear and Momma Bear and the baby bears all in the White House!

CANTWELL

(From bedroom)

Where's my electric razor?

MABEL

I'll get it! *(She goes quickly into bedroom)* I'll just start putting on my clothes and . . .

(She finds the razor and gives it to him)

CANTWELL

Where's that last Gallup poll?

MABEL

I think Don Blades got it. Anyway, you're two per cent higher than last week with twelve per cent undecided. Merwin gained one per cent and Russell's lost two per cent.

CANTWELL

And Red China?

MABEL

(Promptly)

Forty-seven per cent against recognition. Twenty-three per cent in favor. Thirty per cent don't know. I'm wearing the green organza tonight, the one from Neiman Marcus, Allan Bates sent me. I think it looks real summery and nice . . .

CANTWELL

(*Frowns*)

That's not enough in favor. Russell's a fool making an issue out of China this soon . . .

(MABEL *removes her dressing gown and starts to get into her dress*)

MABEL

I had my hair done this morning by the man in the hotel; he's very nice but terribly swishy. Anyway he didn't get the curls too tight. . . . At least I don't think so. He said Alice Russell had her hair done, too. (*Unnoticed by* MABEL, CANTWELL *goes into living room, sits at desk, turns on electric razor and reads a newspaper*) He said she refuses to entertain the thought of using so much as a rinse. Well, bully for her! She looks easily ten years older than she is. (*Frowns*) Joe, do you think I've gained weight? Around the hips? Honey, you listenin to me? (*Realizing he is in the other room,* MABEL, *pouting, crosses to living-room door, the back of her dress unzipped*) No, I guess you're not . . . You never listen to poor Mama Bear any more. (*Pause*) Joe? Have you ever been unfaithful to me?

CANTWELL

(*Turns off razor*)

No. Did you see Walter Lippmann this morning? Listen to what that guy says: "The country's affairs will be in good hands should William Russell be our next President." (*Slaps the paper down*) I don't know why I don't appeal to those would-be intellectuals. My image just doesn't project to them like his does. (*Notices* MABEL *at last*) Well, look at you! Just good enough to eat . . . (*He starts to nuzzle her in a bearish way*) Mmmm — mm —

MABEL

(*Happily nuzzled*)

Now what are you doing to me? Don't muss my hair! Now come on! Stop it! And zip me up! (*She turns around. As* JOE *zips her dress, she returns to her theme*) Joe, are you sure you haven't been unfaithful to me maybe just one little time? On one of those junkets? Like that awful one to Paris you took, where the Senators got drunk and Clarence Wetlaw contracted a social disease and Helen Wetlaw was fit to be tied?

CANTWELL

Mabel, honey, there's nobody else. And even if there was, how would I have the time? I operate on a tight schedule. (*Kisses her briefly*) You know that.

(BLADES *enters from corridor door*)

BLADES

Joe, I talked to Hockstader.

CANTWELL

Well?

BLADES

He'll be right down.

CANTWELL

And?

BLADES

Not a clue.

CANTWELL

O.K. Get me that file on Russell. (*To* MABEL, *indicating bed-*

54

room) Honey, you go in there . . . fix your face or something.
The President's on his way down.
> (MABEL *nods and crosses to hall*)

MABEL

Joe . . . play it cool, like the kids say now.

CANTWELL

I will.
> (BLADES *gives him a manila folder*)

BLADES

This ought to do the trick.

CANTWELL

I'll say it will. (*Turns the pages*) Oh, cute. Very cute. How's
the New York delegation?

BLADES

Still split down the middle.

CANTWELL

Well, they won't be split after this.
> (*A sound of excited voices from corridor*)

BLADES

Here he comes. Are you ready?
> (CANTWELL *nods; he takes a position at stage right*)

CANTWELL

All set. (*Warningly*) Don: remember . . . flatter him!
> (BLADES *nods, opens the door.* HOCKSTADER *in evening
> dress pushes his way through a mob of newsmen*)

CANTWELL

Mr. President!

(CANTWELL *beams and crosses to* HOCKSTADER *as* BLADES *shuts out the press*)

HOCKSTADER

Hello, Blades . . . Hi, Joe! (HOCKSTADER *indicates the corridor door*) Well, this ought to start some rumors.

(CANTWELL *is now shaking his hand warmly*)

CANTWELL

Gosh, I'm sorry, sir. We should've arranged for you to come in the back way.

HOCKSTADER

Oh, that's all right. We're gettin near that time anyway. (*Taps coat pocket*) Got my speech right here. My teeth are in and I'm rarin to go. (*Indicates* CANTWELL) What about you? Where's your party suit?

CANTWELL

(*Seriously*)

I have it all timed. It takes me exactly three minutes to get into a tux. Two minutes for an ordinary business suit, and that's including vest.

HOCKSTADER

(*Smiles*)

Well, ain't you a ring-tailed wonder? (*Crosses to bar*) You don't mind if I strike myself a blow for liberty?

CANTWELL

Let me . . . please . . . (*Gestures to* BLADES *to help*) Don!

56

HOCKSTADER

(*Fixes his own drink*)

That's all right. I know Joe doesn't have the habit. People who don't drink never realize how thirsty we old bucks get long round sundown. (*Turns thoughtfully to* CANTWELL) No, sir, you don't drink, you don't smoke, you don't philander; fact, you are about the purest young man I have ever known in public life.

CANTWELL

I try to be.

(HOCKSTADER *crosses to sofa downstage*)

HOCKSTADER

Well, I am a great admirer of virtue, though a somewhat flawed vessel of grace myself.

(HOCKSTADER *sits*)

CANTWELL

Now, Mr. President . . . you're an ideal to us in the party.

(CANTWELL *sits opposite him stage left.* BLADES *is seated stage right*)

HOCKSTADER

(*Dryly*)

Sure, Joe, sure . . . Young man, you've done a remarkable job in the Senate. Most of the time.

CANTWELL

(*Quickly*)

Most of the time?

HOCKSTADER

(*Nods*)

There *have* been moments when I have questioned your methods.

CANTWELL

Well, you have to fight fire with fire, Mr. President.

HOCKSTADER

And the end justifies the means?

CANTWELL

Well, yes, sir. Yes. That is what I believe.

HOCKSTADER

Well, son, I have news for you about both politics and life . . . and may I say the two are *exactly* the same thing? There are no ends, Joe, only means.

CANTWELL

Well, I don't like to disagree with you, sir, but that's just sophistry. I mean . . .

HOCKSTADER

(*Amused*)

Now! None of them two-bit words on poor old Art Hockstader. I'm just an ignorant country boy. All I'm saying is that what matters in our profession . . . which is really life . . . is *how* you do things and *how* you treat people and what you really feel about 'em, *not* some ideal goal for society, or for yourself.

CANTWELL

(*His District-Attorney voice*)

Then am I to assume, Mr. President, from the statement you have just made, that you are against planning anything?

HOCKSTADER

(*Laughs*)

Oh, here it comes! I know that voice! Senator Cantwell, boy

crusader, up there on the TV with these small-time hoodlums cringing before his righteousness.

BLADES
(*To the rescue*)
Now, Mr. President, Joe was *assigned* that Subcommittee. He didn't ask for it . . . and that's a fact.

HOCKSTADER
Sure. Sure. And he just fell into that big issue: how the United States is secretly governed by the Mafia.

CANTWELL
It happened to be true. Any time you want to look at my files, Mr. President . . .

HOCKSTADER
Last time somebody asked me to look at his files, it was Senator McCarthy.

CANTWELL
(*Grimly*)
I hope, sir, you're not comparing me to him.

HOCKSTADER
No . . . no, Joe. You're a much smoother article. After all, you've got an end to which you can justify your means, getting to be President. Poor old McCarthy was just wallowing in headlines . . . sufficient to the day were the headlines thereof. No, you're much brighter, much more ruthless.

CANTWELL
I realize some of my methods upset a lot of people . . .

BLADES
(*Righteously*)
But, Mr. President, if we hadn't been tough we would never have cracked the Mafia the way we did.
(HOCKSTADER *smiles during this*)

CANTWELL
What's so funny about that, sir?

HOCKSTADER
Nothing, only you know and I know and everybody knows . . . except I'm afraid the TV audience . . . that there never was a Mafia like you said. There was no such thing. You just cooked it up.

CANTWELL
(*Dangerously*)
So we're going to get that number, are we? Well, my figures prove . . .

HOCKSTADER
(*Sharply*)
You went after a bunch of poor Sicilian bandits on the lower East Side of New York and pretended they were running all the crime in America. Well, they're not. Of course we have a pretty fair idea who is, but you didn't go after any of them, did you? No, sir, because those big rascals are heavy contributors to political campaigns.

BLADES
(*Beginning*)
Maybe Joe didn't go after all of them, sir . . .

HOCKSTADER

Just barely scratched the surface . . .

CANTWELL

But *you* should talk. J. Edgar Hoover considered you the most morally lax President in his entire career . . .

HOCKSTADER
(*Serenely*)

I reserve my opinion of J. Edgar Hoover for a posthumous memoir or maybe a time capsule to be dug up when he has finally cleansed the republic of undesirables.

CANTWELL

Hoover is a great American!

HOCKSTADER
(*Amused*)

But we're all "great Americans," Joe. (*More seriously*) No, I don't object to your headline-grabbing and crying "Wolf" all the time, that's standard stuff in politics, but it disturbs me you take yourself so seriously. It's par for the course trying to fool the people but it's downright dangerous when you start fooling yourself.

(MABEL CANTWELL, *in the bedroom, has heard voices grow angry. She crosses to the hall and listens at the living-room door*)

CANTWELL
(*Carefully*)

Mr. President, I take myself seriously. Because I am serious. This is important to me. To all of us. Which is why I don't want any little lectures from you on how to be a statesman. And if you really want to know, I think the record of your administration is one of the heaviest loads our party has to carry.

(HOCKSTADER *is on his feet, suddenly furious.* MABEL *enters*)

MABEL

Why, Mr. President! What a nice surprise, your dropping in on us like this!

(HOCKSTADER *regains his composure*)

HOCKSTADER

Well, I was invited down here by this young man for a little conference, and here he is, turning my head with flattery.

MABEL
(*Rapturously*)

Joe admires you, I guess, more than any man in public life.

CANTWELL
(*To* MABEL)

Honey, leave us alone. (*Indicates to* BLADES *that he leave, too*) Don.

(BLADES *exits right*)

MABEL

All right, but Joe, you have to get dressed soon.

CANTWELL

O.K.

MABEL

You certainly look fine, Mr. President, after your little vacation in the hospital . . .

HOCKSTADER

Fit as a fiddle. Never felt better.

(MABEL *goes into connecting hall. She shuts the door. She listens*)

CANTWELL

I'm sorry, sir, flying off the handle like that.

HOCKSTADER

(*Smiles*)

That's O.K. You just got a case of the old pre-convention jitters . . . Now I assume you didn't ask me down here to discuss the virtues of J. Edgar Hoover.

CANTWELL

No, I didn't. (*Awkwardly*) I know you don't like me . . .

HOCKSTADER

Now that you mention it, I don't. I never have.

CANTWELL

And I've never liked your kind of politician. But that's neither here nor there. I don't expect you to come out for me tonight . . .

(HOCKSTADER *crosses to the bar upstage. He fixes himself another drink*)

HOCKSTADER

I should warn you I have often endorsed men I disliked, even mistrusted, because I thought they'd do the job.

(CANTWELL *has gone to the desk. He picks up the file.* HOCKSTADER *suffers a spasm of pain at the bar. He clutches his stomach.* CANTWELL *does not notice this*)

63

CANTWELL

So I have something to show you about your friend William Russell. It's all here in this file. I want you to look at it and . . . (CANTWELL *looks at* HOCKSTADER; *he realizes something is wrong*) What's the matter with you?

HOCKSTADER
(*With difficulty*)

Just . . . had to take one of my pills. (*Takes a pill*) Pep me up. (CANTWELL *nods, goes downstage to sofa. He sits.* HOCKSTADER *looks at him thoughtfully*) Joe, you believe in God, don't you?

CANTWELL
(*Promptly*)

Yes, I do.

HOCKSTADER

And you believe there's a Hereafter? And a Day of Judgment?

CANTWELL
(*Sincerely*)

I do. If I didn't think there was some meaning to all of this I wouldn't be able to go on. I'm a very religious guy, in a funny way.

(CANTWELL *spreads the contents of the folder on the coffee table*)

HOCKSTADER

I'm sure you are. (*Sighs*) Times like this I wish I was. Dying is no fun, let me tell you. And that's what I'm doing.

(CANTWELL *has not been listening*)

CANTWELL
(*Briskly*)

Now it's all here. Psychiatrist reports . . . everything. And don't ask *how* I got it. My means might've been ruthless but for once I think you'll agree the end was worth it.

(HOCKSTADER *is taken aback at being ignored. He comes downstage. He indicates the papers contemptuously*)

HOCKSTADER

What is all this . . . crap?

CANTWELL

Several years ago *your* candidate, William Russell, had what is known as a nervous breakdown.

HOCKSTADER

I know that.

CANTWELL

He was raving mad for almost a year.

HOCKSTADER

He was not raving mad. It was exhaustion from overwork . . .

CANTWELL

That was the press release. The real story's right here . . .

HOCKSTADER

I know the real story.

CANTWELL

Then you know it's political dynamite. A full report on his

mental state. How he deserted his wife, how their marriage has always been a phony, a political front . . .

HOCKSTADER

I won't begin to speculate on how you got hold of this . . .

CANTWELL

And all the big words are there, manic depressive, paranoid pattern, attempted suicide . . .

HOCKSTADER

He never attempted suicide.

CANTWELL

I'm sorry. It says right here that he did. See? (*Points to page*) There. Suicidal tendencies . . .

HOCKSTADER

We've all got suicidal *tendencies*. But he never tried to kill himself.

CANTWELL

But the point is he *could*.

HOCKSTADER

I thought you said he *did* try.

CANTWELL

I did not say he did. I said he could. And then all that combined with playing around with women . . .

HOCKSTADER

So what?

CANTWELL

I suppose you find promiscuity admirable?

66

HOCKSTADER

I couldn't care less. I was brought up on a farm and the lesson of the rooster was not entirely lost on me. A lot of men need a lot of women and there are worse faults, let me tell you.

CANTWELL
(*Suspiciously*)
What do you mean by that?

HOCKSTADER

Just that there are rumors about every public man. Why, when I was in the White House they used to say I had paresis, and how I was supposed to be keepin this colored girl over in Alexandria, silliest damn stories you ever heard but it gave a lot of people a lot of pleasure talkin about it. You know, when that Kinsey fellow wrote that book about how many men were doin this and how many men were doin that, I couldn't help but think how right along with all this peculiar activity there was a hell of a lot of *nothin* goin on!

CANTWELL

All right, leaving the moral issue out, do you think it a good idea to elect a man President who is mentally unstable?

HOCKSTADER

He is not mentally unstable and you know it.

CANTWELL
(*Inexorably*)
A manic depressive? Apt to crack up under stress?
(HOCKSTADER *gets the point*)

67

HOCKSTADER

So that's your little number, is it?

CANTWELL

(*Evenly*)

If Russell doesn't withdraw before Wednesday, I am going to see that every delegate gets a copy of this psychiatric report and I am going to challenge Russell openly. I'm going to ask him if he really feels that a man with his mental record should be President of the United States. Frankly, if I were he, I'd pull out before this (*Indicates papers*) hits the fan.

HOCKSTADER

Well, you are *not* Russell . . . to state the obvious. And he might say in rebuttal that after his breakdown he served a right rough period as Secretary of State and did not show the strain in any way.

CANTWELL

One of the psychiatrists reports that this pattern of his is bound to repeat itself. He is bound to have another breakdown.

HOCKSTADER

You and your experts! You know as well as I do those head-doctors will give you about as many different opinions as you want on any subject.

CANTWELL

(*Reasonably*)

I realize that, which is why I am going to propose that he be examined, before Wednesday, by a nonpartisan group of psychiatrists to determine if he is sane.

68

HOCKSTADER

You know he won't submit to that.

CANTWELL

If he doesn't, that means he has something to hide.

HOCKSTADER

Wow! You sure play rough, don't you?

CANTWELL

I regard this as a public service. (*Urgently*) Look, I'm not asking you to support me. I don't even *want* your support. But I do want you to think twice before endorsing a man who is known to be psychopathic.

HOCKSTADER

You got it figured, of course, that even to hint that a man's not right in his head will be enough to knock him off? When do you plan to throw this at him?

CANTWELL

Tomorrow.

HOCKSTADER

And of course you've waited for the last minute so he won't have a chance to clear himself before the convention starts. That's right smart.

CANTWELL

(*Not listening*)

We'll have to work out some way for him to get out of the race gracefully. I thought maybe he could say . . . well, nervous exhaustion . . . doesn't feel up to the rigors of a campaign, something like that.

HOCKSTADER

And if he doesn't withdraw "gracefully"?

CANTWELL

(*Taps folder*)

This will be circulated. And I will demand he be examined by psychiatrists.

HOCKSTADER

I suppose you realize you are now open to the same kind of treatment.

CANTWELL

I have nothing to hide in my private or public life.

HOCKSTADER

Are you absolutely certain?

CANTWELL

(*Carefully*)

Just . . . try . . . anything.

HOCKSTADER

Well, looks like we're goin to have an ugly fight on our hands. Yes, sir, a real ugly fight. (*Crosses to upstage door. He turns*) So now I am going to let you have it. And when I finish with you, my boy, you will know what it is like to get in the ring with an old-time killer. I am going to have your political scalp and hang it on my belt, along with a lot of others.

CANTWELL

(*Dangerously*)

Don't mix with me, Hockstader.

HOCKSTADER

You can't touch me. But I can send you back to the insurance business. (*He removes his speech from his pocket, almost sadly*) And just think! I was going to endorse *you* for President.

CANTWELL

I don't believe you.

HOCKSTADER

It's not that I mind your bein a bastard, don't get me wrong there . . . It's your bein such a *stupid* bastard I object to.

(*Contemptuously,* HOCKSTADER *tosses the speech at* CANTWELL's *feet. Then he turns and exits to the corridor, flinging the door open. Flash-bulbs go off. As* HOCKSTADER *disappears into the crowd of newsmen,* CANTWELL *picks up the speech and starts to read*)

CURTAIN

ACT TWO

ACT TWO

SCENE ONE

The Russell suite. The next afternoon. A delegation is being shown out by RUSSELL *and* JENSEN. *They pump hands. Russell placards are waved. At the bar stands* SENATOR CAR-LIN, *a ponderous politician of the prairies.*

JENSEN

O.K., gentlemen . . . we'll see you tomorrow, in the convention hall.

DELEGATE
(*To* RUSSELL, *warmly*)

Bill, we'll nominate you on the first ballot tomorrow . . . and that's a promise . . .

RUSSELL
(*Smiles*)

If nominated, I will run. If elected, I will serve. Thanks.

JENSEN
(*To the last* DELEGATE)

We'll be in touch with you . . . (*To* RUSSELL) Well, what do you think?

RUSSELL

Looks all right. Nobody's mentioned mental health yet.

75

CARLIN

What *did* you fellows think of Hockstader's speech last night?
(*Both* RUSSELL *and* JENSEN *turn, startled*)

RUSSELL

Senator Carlin! I thought you'd left . . .

CARLIN

No. Just stayed to fix myself a snort, if you don't mind. Now about Hockstader's speech last night . . .

RUSSELL

Well, I was as surprised as anybody.

CARLIN

You thought he was going to endorse you?

JENSEN
(*Quickly*)

We certainly did.

CARLIN

And then the old man just got up and talked plain double talk . . .

JENSEN

At least he didn't endorse Cantwell.
(JENSEN *goes off left*)

CARLIN

No. He didn't endorse *nobody*. For a minute I thought he was going to surprise us and come out for John Merwin, just to be ornery. Now I hear you were with the old man later on last night.

76

What's he up to? My boys think a lot of old Art and they'll go along with him . . .

CARLIN

RUSSELL

We were having a council of war, I guess you'd call it.

CARLIN

They say Joe's got something on you, something pretty bad.

RUSSELL

Something untrue. And frankly I'm not very worried. I'm a lot more worried about the labor plank in the platform . . .

CARLIN
(*Exasperated*)

Oh, Christ, Bill! Lay off labor, will you? You got their vote now, so don't go stirring up a lot of snakes. After all, *you're* the liberal candidate . . .

RUSSELL

What is a liberal, Senator?
(RUSSELL *crosses to bedroom, picks up dictionary, returns to living room, thumbing pages*)

CARLIN
(*Groans*)

And I thought Adlai Stevenson was a pain in the neck. A liberal is a . . . well, you, Bill Russell, are a liberal, that's what a liberal is. You.

RUSSELL

According to the dictionary a liberal is one who "favors changes and reforms tending in the direction of further democracy." Well,

I am in favor of further democracy for the unions' rank and file . . .

CARLIN

Bill, please . . . I'm just a poor dumb party hack . . .

RUSSELL

I'm sorry, Senator. The terrible thing about running for President is you become a compulsive talker, forever answering questions no one has asked you.

CARLIN

Well, let me ask *you* a question. Would you consider offering the Vice-President nomination to Cantwell?

RUSSELL

No.

CARLIN

(*Sourly*)

For a compulsive talker, you sure don't have much to say on that subject. (*Sighs*) Jeez, I hate an open convention. You can't ever tell what's going to happen!

RUSSELL

(*Smiles*)

They're never that open.

CARLIN

I suppose we better try for a Catholic . . . that seems to be the big thing this year . . . for *second* place, that is. (JENSEN *returns with papers*) Bill, *don't* make things tough for yourself! You got the nomination now so leave the controversial things alone.

RUSSELL

I can't help it. I am driven by a mad demon, by some imp of the perverse . . . (CARLIN *looks at him narrowly.* JENSEN *gives him a warning look*) That is, I am *compelled* to say what I think.

CARLIN

O.K., but try to lay off stuff like Red China, especially when you know Henry Luce is an absolute nut on China and you don't want to lose *Time* and *Life* when they're already behind you in the interests of good government and all that crap. . . . So keep Henry Luce happy, will you? Once you're President, you can eat with chopsticks for all anybody cares.

RUSSELL

I will be diplomatic.

CARLIN

You know, Cantwell's releasing a statement today. To all the delegates. He says it'll knock you off.

RUSSELL

We're ready for him. He may be the master of the half truth and the insinuation, but we've got the facts.

CARLIN

And the *whole* truth?

RUSSELL

(*Lightly*)

No man has the whole truth.

CARLIN

Oh, brother! Good luck, Bill. Let me know if there's anything

I can do for you. I'm with you one hundred per cent, in spite of your damned dictionary.

RUSSELL

Thank you, Senator.
(CARLIN *goes.* RUSSELL *goes into the bedroom and sits wearily on the bed*)

RUSSELL

Dick, where's Dr. Artinian?

JENSEN

On his way from the airport.
(JENSEN *enters bedroom, sits on chair opposite the bed*)

RUSSELL

And Hockstader?

JENSEN

Talking to delegates. . . . Bill, I've finally got a line on Cantwell. I got some real dirt . . .

RUSSELL

Of all the stunts, this is the craziest! If you'll excuse my obsessive use of words like "mad" and "crazy."

JENSEN

You could've cut the air with a knife when you made that crack about being "driven by a mad demon" . . .
(RUSSELL *has started his walk across the carpet*)

RUSSELL

Well, they re-elected Eisenhower after a heart attack and an ileitis operation . . . didn't seem to hurt him.

JENSEN

But there was never any question about his mind or his judgment being affected. (RUSSELL *has completed his walk*) Well? What's the score?

RUSSELL

(*Smiles*)

I still get it on the first ballot but it was a near miss: I nearly stepped on that leaf, the one by the table . . . it's a bitch. (*Indicates newspaper*) What about your daily horoscope?

JENSEN

(*From memory*)

"A.M. Fine for getting apparel in order. P.M. do not quarrel with loved one." Bill, you may have to pull a Nixon.

RUSSELL

And what does "pull a Nixon" mean?

JENSEN

Go on television. And cry on the nation's shoulder. With *two* cocker spaniels.

RUSSELL

And tell them I'm not crazy? No. I admit it's possible to look directly into a camera and persuade the people I won't steal their money, but I promise you, Dick, you can't look a camera in the face and say, "Honest, I'm not crazy. I just had a nervous breakdown like any regular fellow might." No, it won't work.

JENSEN

Why not?

81

RUSSELL

Because it won't. And even if it did, I couldn't do it. (*Chuckles*) I might . . . laugh. It's too idiotic.
(ALICE *enters from corridor door*)

RUSSELL

How was the meeting?

ALICE

I made a speech. At least I started to read the one Dick gave me. Then halfway through I gave up and made my own speech, and do you know what? It was terrible! (*Suddenly grave*) What's happened?

RUSSELL

Dr. Artinian's on his way to Philadelphia. He's going to tell the press that I am not and never was insane.

ALICE

It gets worse and worse, doesn't it?

RUSSELL

Yes, it does.
(JENSEN *rises, crosses to connecting-hall door*)

JENSEN

I've got to get back to work. Here. (*He puts a schedule on the other twin bed*) We have Ohio in twenty minutes. Then one more go at California.

RUSSELL

Send Dr. Artinian in the second he gets here.
(JENSEN *nods, exits left*)

ALICE

Does this mean they could publish everything about us? Our marriage and . . . *everything?*

RUSSELL

Yes.

(ALICE *sits on the same twin bed as* RUSSELL; *they are back to back*)

ALICE

Will they?

RUSSELL

I don't know. I think it's just a bluff right now, to frighten me.

ALICE

It frightens me. I should hate to think of the children reading all that about us. Oh, it is filthy . . . filthy!

RUSSELL

Do you want me to quit?

ALICE

(*A pause*)

No.

(RUSSELL *puts his hand on* ALICE's; *she smiles*)

ALICE

How very odd!

RUSSELL

What?

ALICE

Do you realize that this is the first time you've touched me when there wasn't a camera or someone in the room?

(*There is a tense moment; then he pats her hand briskly and rises; he picks up the sheet of paper* JENSEN *left on the other bed*)

RUSSELL

Well, here's your schedule. Your next appointment is . . . Oh, my God, I forgot all about this!

ALICE

(*Grimly*)

I haven't. Mabel Cantwell and I face the press together. Can I get out of it?

RUSSELL

No. Better not.

ALICE

Then I'll get ready. We're meeting in her suite. She made the point very tactfully over the phone that (ALICE *lapses into deep Mabelese*) accordin to protocol the wife of a reignin Senator outranks the wife of a former Secretary of State.

RUSSELL

(*Equally Southern*)

Well, bless my soul!

(ALICE *goes.* DR. ARTINIAN, *a distinguished-looking psychiatrist . . . the first to be depicted in the American theater without a Mittel-Europa accent . . . enters with* JENSEN *from left.* RUSSELL *crosses living room to greet him, just as*

84

the buzzer from the corridor sounds. JENSEN *hurries to corridor door)*

RUSSELL

Robert, I'm glad you could get away like this . . .

ARTINIAN

I had to.
(JENSEN *opens corridor door to admit* HOCKSTADER, *who darts in while* JENSEN *pushes back the press*)

RUSSELL

Dr. Artinian . . . President Hockstader.
(HOCKSTADER *and* ARTINIAN *shake hands*)

HOCKSTADER

You Bill's head-doctor?

ARTINIAN

That's right. And I'm a very great admirer of yours, Mr. President.

HOCKSTADER

Well, I'm *not* an admirer of yours. Why don't you people keep your damned files where nobody can get at 'em?

ARTINIAN

We do. Or we thought we did. Apparently somebody from Cantwell's office bribed one of our nurses . . . they got the entire case history.

RUSSELL

Robert, in one hour Cantwell's releasing that file on me. Now I know this sounds silly, but when he does, I want you to meet the press and tell them I am *not* mentally unstable.

ARTINIAN

Of course I will. You don't know how guilty I feel about this.
(ARTINIAN *turns to exit left with* JENSEN)

HOCKSTADER
(*Suddenly*)

He *is* all right, isn't he?

ARTINIAN
(*Smiles*)

Mr. Russell is one of the sanest men I ever have known.

HOCKSTADER

Then what's all that stuff about suicide tendencies and manic-mania or whatever you call it?

ARTINIAN

Just technical phrases which may sound sinister to a layman. He is certainly *not* a manic depressive. Anyone's psychological profile could be made to sound . . . damaging.

RUSSELL
(*Lightly*)

In the South a candidate for sheriff once got elected by claiming that his opponent's wife had been a thespian.

JENSEN

We'll find a room for you here, Doctor. And I'll get somebody to help you with your statement.

86

ARTINIAN

Thank you. I also brought the Institute's lawyer with me. By way of making amends, Bill, we're filing suit against Cantwell for theft . . .

HOCKSTADER
(*Pleased*)

That's the ticket. Go to it, Doc.

ARTINIAN
(*To* RUSSELL)

I'll be ready when you want me.

RUSSELL
(*Warmly*)

Many thanks, Robert.
(ARTINIAN *and* JENSEN *go off left.* RUSSELL *is about to follow when* HOCKSTADER *stops him*)

HOCKSTADER

Bill, I want you to myself a minute. Now what's this I hear about you not goin on the TV?

RUSSELL

I can't.

HOCKSTADER

How the hell you goin to fight this thing if you don't?

RUSSELL

Dr. Artinian . . .

HOCKSTADER
(*Disgust*)

Dr. Artinian! That's just *one* doctor. They'll say he's a friend of yours. Cantwell's going to insist they have half the medical profession look you over between now and tomorrow . . . (*Pacing happily*) Oh, I tell you, Bill, I feel wonderful! Up all night . . . on the go all morning, seein delegates . . . I tell you there is *nothin* like a dirty low-down political fight to put the roses in your cheeks.

RUSSELL
(*Concerned*)

How *do* you feel?

HOCKSTADER

Immortal! Now a lot of the delegates know that somethin's up. They don't know what . . .

RUSSELL
(*Abruptly*)

Art, why didn't you endorse me last night?

HOCKSTADER
(*Awkwardly*)

Look, Bill, this isn't easy to say, but you might as well know: I came to Philadelphia to nominate Cantwell.

RUSSELL
(*Nods*)

I knew that.

HOCKSTADER
(*Taken aback*)

You did! How?

RUSSELL

(*Wryly*)

Prince Hamlet has second sight. He sees motives as well as ghosts upon the battlement.

HOCKSTADER

Guess I ain't as sly as I figured I was.

RUSSELL

Did you decide to help me now because of what Joe's doing? Bringing up that breakdown business?

HOCKSTADER

No. No. Matter of fact . . . speaking as a professional politician . . . I kind of admire what he's doing. It's clever as all hell. No, Joe Cantwell lost me because he wasn't smart. He made a mistake. He figured I was goin to back you when I wasn't. You got my message. Joe didn't. Now that's a serious error. Shows he don't understand character and a President if he don't understand anything else has got to understand people. Then he got flustered when I needled him. A President don't get flustered when a man gives him the needle. He keeps a straight face, like poker. (*Smiles*) Like you're doin right now. But what does Joe do? He don't run scared; he runs terrified. He fires off a cannon to kill a bug. And that is just plain dumb and I mean to knock him off . . . which means that you, I guess, are goin to be our next President.

RUSSELL

President . . . but by default. Because you still have your doubts about me, don't you?

HOCKSTADER

Yes, I still have my doubts. Bill, I want a strong President . . .

89

RUSSELL

An immoral President?

(HOCKSTADER *turns away disgustedly*)

HOCKSTADER

They hardly come in any other size.

RUSSELL

You don't believe that . . .

(JENSEN *enters with a plump, bald, nervous man of forty-odd who resembles an unmade studio couch*)

JENSEN

This is Sheldon Marcus.

HOCKSTADER

(*Irritably*)

Who the hell is Sheldon Marcus? (HOCKSTADER *turns, sees that the man is already in the room; he flashes a Presidential smile and, hand outstretched, crosses to* MARCUS) If you'll excuse me, sir?

MARCUS

That's all right. I . . . I never thought I'd meet a President. (MARCUS *rubs his shaken hand against his trouser leg*) My hands sweat. I . . . I'm nervous, I guess. You see, I just now came in from Wilmington, where I live, outside Wilmington's actually where I live, a suburb you never heard of called . . .

RUSSELL

Dick, what's this all about? I'm Bill Russell.

JENSEN

Mr. Marcus served in the army with Joe Cantwell . . .

HOCKSTADER

In the army? (*Starts to beam with anticipation*) Ah . . . ah
. . . *Now* we're gettin somewhere. Well, what was it? Was he a
member of the Ku Klux Klan? The Communist Party? Or did he
run away when the guns went off?

MARCUS

Well, sir, Mr. President, sir, uh, we weren't anywheres around
where there were guns . . .

JENSEN

They were both in the Aleutians. On the island of Adak. The
Quartermaster Corps.

MARCUS

(*Nods*)

We were there for a year, well, maybe more like eighteen
months for me and, oh, maybe sixteen, seventeen months for Joe,
he came there February '43 and I got there . . .

RUSSELL

(*To* JENSEN)

Dick, what are you trying to prove?

HOCKSTADER

Now shush, Bill. And let's hear the dirt, whatever it is.

MARCUS

Well . . . Joe . . . (*Pauses in an agony of embarrassment*)
Oh, I sure hate talking about him, telling something so awful . . .

JENSEN

I had a lead on this months ago. I finally tracked it down. . . .
Tell them, Mr. Marcus.

91

MARCUS

Well, Joe Cantwell was a captain and I was a captain and Joe Cantwell was . . . was . . . well, he was . . . you know how it is sometimes when there's all those men together and . . . and . . .

JENSEN

And no female companionship . . .

MARCUS

That's right, though we had some nurses later on, but not enough to make much difference. I mean there were all those men . . .

JENSEN
(*Helpfully*)

And no women.

RUSSELL
(*Irritated*)

Oh, for Christ's sake, Dick, stop it, will you?

HOCKSTADER
(*Soothingly*)

Now . . . now, let's not get ahead of ourselves.

RUSSELL

You know Joe isn't that, and if he was, so what?

HOCKSTADER

I find this very interesting. Mr. Marcus . . . Captain Marcus, I should say . . .

MARCUS

(*Gabbling*)

I was a major, actually, promoted just before my discharge in '46. I'm in the reserve . . . the *in*active reserve . . . but if there was another war I would be . . .

HOCKSTADER

(*Through him*)

Major Marcus, am I to understand by the way you are beating slowly around the bush that Joe Cantwell is what . . . when I was a boy . . . we called a de-generate?

MARCUS

(*Relieved to have the word said*)

Yes, sir, Mr. President, sir, that's just what I mean . . .

RUSSELL

(*Amused in spite of himself*)

I don't believe it! Nobody with that awful wife and those ugly children could be anything but normal!

HOCKSTADER

Bill! Patience. Whether *you* believe it or not is beside the point.

RUSSELL

And even if it were true I'm damned if I'd smear him with something like that . . .

HOCKSTADER
(*Patiently and slowly*)

Bill, I, like you, am a tolerant man. I *personally* do not care if Joe Cantwell enjoys deflowering sheep by the light of a full moon. But I *am* interested in finding a way to stop him cold.

RUSSELL

Damn it, Art, this is exactly the kind of thing I went into politics to stop! The business of gossip instead of issues, personalities instead of policies. . . . We've got enough on Cantwell's *public* life to defeat him without going into his private life which is nobody's business!

HOCKSTADER
(*Sharply*)

Any more than yours is?

RUSSELL

Any more than mine is.

HOCKSTADER

But Cantwell *is* using your private life . . .

RUSSELL

All the more reason for my *not* using his. I'm not Cantwell.

HOCKSTADER
(*Reasonably*)

But nobody's used anything *yet*.

RUSSELL

Look here, Art, you are *not* my campaign manager. I am the one running for President, not you. (*To* JENSEN, *grimly*) And as for you, Dick . . .

JENSEN
(*Growing desperate*)
Bill, at least *listen* to the man.

RUSSELL
No!

HOCKSTADER
I'm beginnin to wonder if maybe I'm tryin to help the wrong team.

RUSSELL
(*Losing control*)
Perhaps you are. Perhaps you'd be happier with Cantwell, helping him throw his mud! (*A tense silence.* HOCKSTADER *remains impassive.* RUSSELL *recovers himself quickly. He is contrite*) Art, I'm sorry. I didn't mean that.

HOCKSTADER
(*Amused*)
Observe how I kept a straight face while being insulted?

RUSSELL
You know that I only meant . . .

HOCKSTADER
(*Through him*)
Yes, I know. (*Wheedling*) Now, Bill, as a favor to an old man in his . . . sunset years, will you just listen to Major Marcus? That's all. Just listen.

RUSSELL
All right, Art. I'll listen. But only as a favor to . . . to a friend.

HOCKSTADER

That's fine, Bill. You just relax now and let events take their course. (HOCKSTADER *crosses to the dazed* MARCUS) After all, how often does a million dollars (*Pats* MARCUS) drop in your lap? Not to mention the Presidency. (*Propels* MARCUS *to a chair downstage*) Sit down, Major Marcus, sit down. Please. Make yourself comfortable. Fact, I will mix you a drink myself with these old skilled fingers, and while I do you will tell us your story. (*Crosses to bar*) Omitting no details, no matter how sordid.

(RUSSELL *turns upstage, revolted*)

MARCUS

Well, Mr. President, there was this guy up on Adak, and his name was Fenn, Bob Fenn. That is, *Robert* Fenn. (*Light starts to fade*) I don't know his middle initial but I guess it's all there in the record, how this Lieutenant Fenn . . .

CURTAIN

ACT TWO

Scene Two

The Cantwell suite. A few minutes later. MABEL, ALICE *and* MRS. GAMADGE *sit in a row on the sofa in the living room.* MRS. GAMADGE *is in a long evening dress with a vast corsage.* REPORTERS *and* CAMERAMEN *are winding up a press conference.* BLADES *hovers, directs.*

BLADES

All right, boys . . . come on . . . that's enough . . . our girls have got a lot to do . . .

REPORTER 1

Mrs. Russell, where are your sons now?

ALICE

They . . . well, one's in Watch Hill and the other's traveling . . . he's in Europe. I wish now we had them here, for the experience.

(*A flash-bulb goes off*)

MABEL

Oh, I blinked my eyes! (*To* REPORTER 1 *gaily*) Joe and I were going to bring our girls to Philadelphia but then we decided, no, this sort of thing is just too hectic for children . . .

97

REPORTER 2

Mrs. Russell . . . how's *Mr.* Russell today?

ALICE

He's just fine . . .

REPORTER 3

There has been a rumor that he is not in the very best of health.

ALICE
(*Growing steely*)
I have never seen him in better health.

MABEL

My Joe just blossoms during a campaign! On the go all the time! I don't know *where* he gets the energy.

ALICE

In fact, my husband . . .

MRS. GAMADGE
(*Through her*)
Joe Cantwell is a real dynamo!

ALICE
(*A second try*)
In fact, my husband . . .

MABEL

I sometimes think Joe has got nerves of iron. Nothing ever seems to upset him.

MRS. GAMADGE
(*Nods*)
He has a great inner calm, which is almost spiritual.

ALICE
(*Gamely*)
My husband . . .

BLADES
O.K. That's it, fellows . . .
(*The* REPORTERS *start to go*)

REPORTER 3
(*To* ALICE)
What do you think's going to happen tomorrow? Do you think
Mr. Russell's got it on the first ballot?

ALICE
I certainly hope so!

MABEL
(*Butter would not melt, etc.*)
Well, as for me, I just hope the best man wins! I mean for the
country and everything.

MRS. GAMADGE
Amen to that!
(BLADES *follows* REPORTERS *out into corridor*)

BLADES
Good day, ladies!
(*The three women are alone.* MRS. GAMADGE *sighs gust-ily*)

MABEL

Well, *that* was an ordeal, wasn't it, Mrs. Russell?

ALICE

I'm sure it wasn't for you. (*Afraid this sounded too sharp, amends*) I mean you've done so much of this . . . kind of thing. (*Rises*) I have to go.

(MABEL *gets to her feet quickly*)

MABEL

Oh, stay and have a drink . . . just for a minute. I don't have anything to do till (*Looks at schedule*) . . . till four-fifteen. So let's play hooky!

ALICE

I'm afraid I have an appointment in fifteen minutes.

MRS. GAMADGE

They have us girls on timetables just like trains. Will you look at me? (*She rises*) All ready to moderate the fashion show at five o'clock.

(MRS. GAMADGE *crosses to bar for a Coca Cola, which she drinks with a straw*)

MABEL

(*Cozily*)

It's a shame we couldn't do everything together, instead of first you meetin one group and then me meetin the same group . . . What can I fix you?

(MABEL *makes herself a drink*)

ALICE

Nothing, thanks. It's too early for me.

(MRS. GAMADGE *is back on the sofa, reading a newspaper*)

MRS. GAMADGE

Well, didn't Art Hockstader surprise everybody last night?

MABEL

Personally, I think he's an old meanie the way he's holding out.
And you know why? (*Indicates newspaper*) Publicity! He absolutely revels in the limelight. . . . Oh, Mrs. Russell, I don't believe you've seen my children.

ALICE

I've seen pictures of them. They're very . . . pretty.
(MABEL *holds up a photograph*)

MABEL

That's Gladys there, the oldest . . . with the braces on her
teeth. I'm afraid they're all going to have to have braces and Lord
knows *where* they got those teeth from. Both Joe and I have perfect teeth, and oh! what a fortune it is having children's teeth
straightened! Do you have a picture of your boys?

ALICE

No. Not with me . . .

MRS. GAMADGE

So good-looking . . .

MABEL

Yes! That was a nice spread on them in *Life*. Such *warm* pictures! You and Mr. Russell certainly get a lot of coverage from
Life, much more than we do.

ALICE

Oh? I thought we were neck and neck.

MABEL

No. I'm afraid Joe and I must simply forget Mr. Luce. You're *his* candidate. For the time being. Oh, come on, sit down. (*Affectionately*) I do like the way you do your hair.

ALICE

Oh? Well . . .

MABEL

You look so like this English teacher I had at State College. A wonderful woman in every way . . .

ALICE

Thank you. But I'm afraid I'm not wonderful . . .

MABEL

Now . . . no false modesty! You are wonderful *and* courageous. I always say Alice Russell is the most courageous woman in public life, don't I, Sue-Ellen?

(MRS. GAMADGE, *immersed in her paper, nods*)

ALICE
(*Curiously*)

In what way, courageous?

MABEL

Why, that committee you were on!

MRS. GAMADGE
(*Suddenly alert*)

Committee? *What* committee?

MABEL

(*Ready for the kill*)

You know — in New York City, the one where you did all that work for *birth control.*

MRS. GAMADGE

(*Horror*)

Birth control! I didn't know that.

ALICE

Well, it *was* twenty years ago. And of course I'm not supposed to mention it now . . . (*To* MABEL) as *you* know.

MRS. GAMADGE

I should hope not! You'll have the Catholics down on us like a ton of bricks. The rhythm cycle, yes (*Makes a vague circular motion with her hand*), but anything else . . . is out.

MABEL

Of course I'm against any kind of artificial means of birth control except where it's a matter of health maybe, but believe me I think it took the courage of a lion to be in favor of people using these contraceptive things when you're in public life. Of course I guess you didn't know then your husband would be running for President one day and when you do that you just can't afford to offend a lot of nice people who vote.

ALICE

I realize that. We must offend no one. Of course, if you offend no one, you don't please anyone very much either, do you? But I suppose that is an occupational hazard in politics. We are all interchangeably inoffensive.

(*There is a pause*)

103

MRS. GAMADGE

Well, now!

MABEL

(*Overlapping*)

Well, hooray for Mrs. Russell! Do you know, you sounded just like your husband then? Didn't she, Sue-Ellen? Didn't she sound just like Bill Russell when he's being witty and profound and way over our poor heads!

ALICE

(*Rising*)

I'd like to think intelligence was contagious. But I'm afraid it isn't, at least in my case. Bill has the brains. I'm not awfully quick.

MABEL

Oh, yes, you are, honey!

ALICE

I've really got to go.

(ALICE *turns upstage.* MRS. GAMADGE *and* MABEL *follow her*)

MRS. GAMADGE

You girls are an absolute inspiration to the American woman, *and I mean it* . . . each in your different way.

ALICE

Thank you very much . . . for that.

MABEL

(*One last shot*)

Oh, by the way, how *is* Mr. Russell's health? I mean *really?* I thought he looked so peaked last night at the dinner and someone did say . . .

ALICE

(*Grimly*)

The reporters are gone, Mrs. Cantwell. You know as well as I do he's perfectly all right. Good-by.

MRS. GAMADGE

'By.

(ALICE *goes*)

MABEL

Well . . . listen to her! "The reporters are gone, Mrs. Cantwell!" If she wasn't so high and mighty she'd take the hint and start saying right now he isn't feeling good so that when he has to pull out there'd be some preparation . . .

(MABEL *goes into bedroom and flops onto the rumpled bed*)

MRS. GAMADGE

(*Following her*)

Mabel, I don't like anything about what Joe's doing. It's plain dirty and I should warn you: I'm a loyal party worker and I'll see that the women are all behind Bill Russell.

MABEL

Under him is more their usual position. It's just sex, sex, sex, morning, noon and night with that Bill Russell.

MRS. GAMADGE

Now, Mabel, unless you were in the room, how would you know?

MABEL

I read that report. Bill Russell is a neurotic who has had a breakdown and his sex life is certainly not normal. Sleeping around with all those women is just plain immature. And we don't want an immature President, do we?

MRS. GAMADGE

We've had some very good Presidents who have slept around a lot more than Bill Russell ever did. And in the White House, too.
(BLADES, CANTWELL *and* CARLIN *enter living room from corridor*)

MABEL

(*Hears them*)
Here come the men!

MRS. GAMADGE

And I must get back to the women. (*She is about to leave through the corridor door when she is surprised to see* CARLIN. *She comes into the living room*) Hello, Senator Carlin. Didn't expect to see you *here*.

CARLIN

Just happened to be in the neighborhood.
(CANTWELL *comes up behind* MRS. GAMADGE *and kisses the back of her neck. She squeals*)

CANTWELL

Hi, Sue-Ellen!

MRS. GAMADGE

(*Quickly recovered*)
Joe, I hope you don't mind if I take the bull by the horns and

106

tell you right now that anything to do with *private* lives is out in politics.

CANTWELL

I couldn't agree more.

MRS. GAMADGE

That's an unwritten law and it's a good one. Once you throw at a man that he has a mistress or an illegitimate child or something like that you get sympathy for him. (*Sadly*) I don't know why but you do. You also make yourself vulnerable because nobody's a saint. Not even you, Joe. So keep what you men do *in* bed *out* of politics. (*She goes, waving gaily*) 'By, Joe. 'By, Bill. 'By, Mabel.

CANTWELL
(*To* BLADES)

Photostats ready?

BLADES

All neatly bound. Six hundred copies to be released to the delegates at three-thirty P.M. Russell's doctor is in town. That means there's going to be some kind of a statement.

CANTWELL
(*Nods*)

He's going to fight.

CARLIN

Aren't you fellows afraid of getting into trouble? Stealing medical records?

BLADES
(*Quickly*)

We didn't steal them.

CANTWELL

They were given to us. *Pro bono publico.* Now just look at
this . . . (CANTWELL *shows* CARLIN *the file. The phone rings in
living room.* MABEL *answers it*)

MABEL

Yes? Who? Oh, Dick Jensen! Yes, Joe's here. Just a sec. You
hold on now. (*To* CANTWELL, *excited*) This is it, honey! They're
giving up!

CANTWELL

(*Takes phone*)

Hi, Dick. Howsa boy? Fine . . . Well, gosh, I don't see how I
can delay much longer. I've told everybody three-thirty. Of
course I'd sort of hoped Bill would be helpful. You know, for the
Party's sake. He could back out so easily now, on this health issue
. . . Yeah? Well, frankly, I don't see any point to postponing . . .
Do I know who? Shel-don Mar-cus? No, I don't think so . . .
Where? (*Harshly*) I want to see Russell. Right now . . . Well,
try and fix it; I'll be right here. (*He hangs up, frowning*)

MABEL

Well, honey, what did he say? Come on now . . . give with
the T.L.!

BLADES

(*Concerned*)

You aren't going to meet with Russell, are you? I thought we'd
decided . . .

CANTWELL

Hold that stuff on Russell.

108

BLADES

Hold it? But we can't. We promised the delegates, three-thirty, we said . . .

CANTWELL

I said hold it.

MABEL
(*Alarm*)

Joe, what's happening?
(CANTWELL *takes the file from* CARLIN)

CANTWELL

Senator, if you'll excuse me . . .

CARLIN

Oh, sure . . . sure . . . Well, good-by, Mrs. Cantwell. (*At the door, he turns to* CANTWELL) You know where to find me . . . *after* three-thirty.
(CARLIN *goes*)

CANTWELL
(*To* BLADES)

Go on. Stop that release.

BLADES
(*Bewildered*)

O.K. . . . you're the boss.
(BLADES *goes off right.* CANTWELL *goes into bedroom. He sits down on the bed, thinking hard.* MABEL *follows, panic beginning*)

MABEL

Joe, what did Russell say to you? What's he doing to you?
(CANTWELL *looks at her blankly.* MABEL *begins to understand*)

MABEL

It's not . . . it's not . . .
(MABEL *stops.* Slowly, CANTWELL *nods.* MABEL, *horrified, sits beside him on the bed, her arm around him*)

MABEL
(*Softly*)

Oh, my God!

CURTAIN

ACT TWO

SCENE THREE

The Russell suite. A few minutes later. MARCUS *has just finished his story.* RUSSELL *stands upstage, back to audience.* HOCKSTADER *starts to rise from sofa to give* MARCUS *some papers he's been studying. He sits back suddenly.* MARCUS *takes the papers from him, as* JENSEN *enters from left.*

JENSEN
(*Excitedly*)
You should've heard Cantwell's voice! First time I've ever heard him stuck! (*To* RUSSELL) He wants to see you. So I said three-thirty and he agreed without a peep. That means *no* announcement to the delegates.

(RUSSELL *turns and crosses to* MARCUS, *who rises*)

RUSSELL
Mr. Marcus, I want to thank you. I know that all this must be as . . . distasteful to you as it is to us.
(RUSSELL *shakes* MARCUS's *hand*)

MARCUS
Well, yes, it is . . . Peggy, my wife, oh, she was fit to be tied when I said I'd talked to Mr. Jensen and was going to come here and see you. She knew the whole story of course. I tell her everything, we have no secrets, Mrs. Marcus and me . . .

111

THE BEST MAN

(RUSSELL *talks through him as he tries to get him off stage left*)

RUSSELL

Yes . . . yes . . . well, many thanks.

JENSEN
(*To* MARCUS)
Would you wait . . . please? In my office? That's the second room, across the hall.

MARCUS

Yes, sir, Mr. Jensen. (*To* HOCKSTADER) I guess this is the biggest moment of my life, meeting you, Mr. President, sir.
(HOCKSTADER, *seated, shakes his hand*)

HOCKSTADER

I expect this *is* the biggest moment of your life, Major. You may have changed history. Excuse me for not getting up.
(MARCUS *is now beginning to enjoy the situation*)

MARCUS

I'll say one thing, I certainly never thought back in '44 when Joe Cantwell and I were on Adak that sixteen years later we'd be here in this hotel with him running for President and me talking to you, sir, who I always admired (*Confidentially*), though I didn't vote for you the second time. You see, Mrs. Marcus felt that . . .

HOCKSTADER
(*Dulcet tones*)
Let your vote, Major Marcus, remain between you and your God.

MARCUS

(*Overcome by this wisdom*)

I guess that's right. Yes. Yes! I'll remember that, sir, I really will . . . (*To* JENSEN, *at door*) I won't have to see Joe, will I?

JENSEN

We hope not.

MARCUS

He's just awful when he's mad . . . he's got this temper. It's like stepping on a snake, stepping on Joe. He can be real scary.

(JENSEN *gets him through the door at last*)

JENSEN

We'll remember that. Thanks a lot. See you in a few minutes. . . . (*To* RUSSELL) Bill, we've done it! We've stopped Joe Cantwell!

RUSSELL

(*Indicates a folder on the coffee table in front of* HOCKSTADER)

I'm not going to use this.

JENSEN

(*Quickly*)

Of course you're not. Except privately. We just take this to Joe and say: "If you make an issue out of this breakdown, *we* make an issue out of a certain bit of court-martial testimony . . ."

(ALICE *enters from corridor*)

RUSSELL

Alice, how did it go?

113

ALICE

My cheeks are tired from smiling for the camera. (*To* HOCK-
STADER) But I must say I'm beginning to like politics, Mr. President, especially when Mrs. Gamadge tells me that I'm an inpira-
tion to American women . . . in my way.

HOCKSTADER

You're an inspiration to me, Miss Alice. Excuse me for not getting up, but would you fetch me some branch water, some just
plain branch water?

ALICE

Of course. (ALICE *goes to bar*) Well, first we talked about
Mabel's children. Then we talked about *my* children. Then we
discussed the role of women in politics. We both agreed that
woman's true place was in the home.

RUSSELL

I'm sure Mrs. Gamadge was eloquent on that subject.

ALICE

Eloquent to the point of obsession. We also agreed that women
should be informed about issues.

HOCKSTADER

Worst damn thing ever happened to this country, giving the
women the vote. Trouble, trouble, trouble. They got no more
sense than a bunch of geese. Give 'em a big smile and a pinch on
the . . . anatomy and you got ten votes.

ALICE

(*Smiles*)
May I quote you, Mr. President?

THE BEST MAN

HOCKSTADER

I will deny ever having made such a vile and un-American statement. (*Takes glass*) Thank you, ma'am.

ALICE

(*To* RUSSELL)

And, finally, there were some pointed references to your health . . .

RUSSELL

Which means they've started. Mentally unstable. Apt to crack up . . . already showing signs of the strain. (*Sighs*) As a matter of fact, I *am* showing signs of strain.

(JENSEN *holds up folder*)

JENSEN

Bill, you can stop them. Right now. We've got the ultimate weapon, massive retaliation as Foster Dulles used to say. (WOMAN AID *opens door at left; she whispers something to* JENSEN, *who nods. She goes.* JENSEN *beams*) We have a visitor.

(BLADES *enters, simulating jauntiness*)

BLADES

Gentlemen . . . Mr. President!

(HOCKSTADER *ignores him*)

RUSSELL

Mr. Blades, contrary to what you may have been told, I'm *not* seeing Joe Cantwell.

BLADES

Oh? But I thought you were. I thought Joe said you'd meet in his room because there aren't so many reporters down there . . .

115

JENSEN
(*To* RUSSELL)
That's right, Bill. I said we'd be right down . . .

RUSSELL
You did!
(BLADES *studies every nuance, trying to get a sense of what is happening*)

BLADES
So I came up to work out some way of getting the Secretary downstairs without anybody seeing him. I checked the service elevator and . . .

HOCKSTADER
Dick, you and that hatchet man there go try out the bathroom route. Through the bedroom. Into the next suite and on down.

BLADES
(*Probing*)
O.K., Mr. President, but if the Secretary *isn't* going downstairs . . .

HOCKSTADER
(*Cold command*)
Get moving, boys.
(JENSEN *indicates for* BLADES *to go with him*)

JENSEN
Come on, Don. This is the dry run.
(*Reluctantly,* BLADES *follows* JENSEN *into the bathroom by way of the bedroom*)

116

RUSSELL
(*To* HOCKSTADER)

I'm not going to do this.

HOCKSTADER

You have to.

ALICE

Do what?

HOCKSTADER

He's got the stuff to knock off Cantwell. Only your lily-livered husband won't go through with it.

ALICE
(*To* RUSSELL)

You can keep them from bringing up all that . . . mental business?

RUSSELL

Maybe . . .

HOCKSTADER

Definitely.

ALICE

Then do it!

RUSSELL

But you don't know what it is I have to do.

ALICE
(*Fiercely*)

I don't care! If you took a gun and shot him I'd help you if I thought that was the only way of keeping our lives . . . private.

HOCKSTADER

Atta girl! Listen to her, Bill. *She* don't run from a fight.

RUSSELL

You know I'm not afraid.

HOCKSTADER

(*Exasperation*)

Then what is wrong with you? Why are you hesitatin *this* time?

RUSSELL

Look, I'm not being righteous and I'm not being fastidious and I do want to win. But how can I, in all conscience, use . . . *this,* even against Cantwell!

HOCKSTADER

(*Furiously*)

I should've stuck with Cantwell! Because listenin to you hem and haw and talk about your conscience is turnin me against you fast. My God, what would happen if you had to make a quick decision in the White House when maybe all our lives depended on whether you could act fast . . . and you just sat there, the way you're doin now, having a high old time with your divided conscience.

RUSSELL

(*Hotly*)

I am *not* divided! I know what I should do and this is *not* it.

HOCKSTADER

Then you don't want to be king of the castle. So stay away from us. Be a saint on your own time. Because you aren't fit to lead anybody.

RUSSELL

(*Stung*)

Why? Because I don't "fire off a cannon to kill a bug"? Because I don't have that quick mindless reaction you seem to confuse with strength? Well, I promise you, there is more danger in a President who acts on animal reflex than in one who is willing to reflect before he acts, who has some vestigial moral sense that goes beyond himself. Don't you see? If I start to fight like Cantwell I lose all meaning . . .

HOCKSTADER

(*Evenly*)

If you don't start to fight, you are finished. Now I am here to tell you this: power is not a toy we give to good children; it is a weapon and the strong man takes it and he uses it and I can assure you he don't turn it on himself nor let another man come at him with a knife that he don't fight back. Well, that knife is at your throat and if you don't go down there and beat Cantwell to the floor with this very dirty stick, then you got no business in this big league, and bastard or not I'll help Joe Cantwell take the whole damned world if he wants it, because it's not for you and never will be!

(*A long moment, broken by the return of* JENSEN *and* BLADES *from the bathroom stage right*)

JENSEN

Well, the coast is clear. We're all set.

BLADES

First, we pass through a suite containing a hosiery salesman and a woman . . . perhaps not his wife.

JENSEN

Definitely not his wife. (*To* RUSSELL) He looks forward to meeting you even though he hopes Cantwell gets the nomination. His companion betrayed no intimacy with the names of either candidate.

BLADES

Then we go down the back stairs and through a room occupied by a widow from Bangor, Maine, who is for Russell . . .

JENSEN

And from there we go to the Cantwell bathroom and then . . . they meet and make history!

BLADES

That's right! Though what's going on beats me.
(HOCKSTADER *has been eying* RUSSELL *coldly during this*)

HOCKSTADER
(*To* RUSSELL, *softly*)

Here's your chance. Your *last* chance. Take it. Go down there. I want a strong President to keep us alive a while longer.
(RUSSELL *makes his decision. He turns to* BLADES *and* JENSEN. *He motions toward the bedroom*)

RUSSELL

Wait for me in there.

BLADES
(*As he goes*)

How are you feeling, Mr. President?

HOCKSTADER

(*Grimly*)

Just fine, considering the alternative.

(*Chuckling,* BLADES *joins* JENSEN *at the bathroom door.* RUSSELL *picks up the documents*)

RUSSELL

(*Half to himself*)

And so, one by one, these compromises, these small corruptions destroy character.

HOCKSTADER

To want power is corruption already. Dear God, you hate yourself for being human.

RUSSELL

No. I only want to *be* human . . . and it is not easy. Once this sort of thing starts, there is no end to it which is why it should never begin. And if *I* start . . . well, Art, how does it end, this sort of thing? *Where* does it end?

HOCKSTADER

In the grave, son, where the dust is neither good nor bad, but just nothing.

(RUSSELL *looks first at* HOCKSTADER; *then at* ALICE. *He goes into the bedroom.* ALICE *follows him; she pauses at the door and watches as* RUSSELL *exits to the bathroom, where* JENSEN *and* BLADES *are waiting*)

ALICE

(*Slowly*)

You are a good man, Mr. President.

HOCKSTADER

I reckon I am, when all's said and done.

(HOCKSTADER, *in pain, tries to take one of his pills; he cannot get his hand to his mouth*)

ALICE

But I don't know if this is the right thing for Bill to do.

(ALICE *continues to look after* RUSSELL, *unaware of* HOCK-STADER'S *pain*)

HOCKSTADER

At least I put a fire under the candidate. I just hope it don't go out . . . Now don't you get alarmed (ALICE *turns on this, startled*) but I want you to go over and pick up that phone and ask for Dr. Latham, he's in the hotel. Tell him I'm in here . . . tell him to come quick, through the back way. Tell him to bring a stretcher because I can't move. (ALICE, *horrified, goes quickly to the telephone*) I'm afraid the old man is just about dead.

CURTAIN

ACT THREE

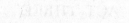

ACT THREE

Scene One

The Cantwell suite. A moment later. CANTWELL *is on the telephone in the living room.* MABEL *is beside him. Both wait, nervously.*

CANTWELL
(At last)
Yes, that's right. The name is Conyers, General Conyers . . . C-o-n-y-e-r-s . . . Yes, this is Senator Cantwell. Yes, it's an emergency. You . . . What? Oh, no! (*To* MABEL) They can't find him!

MABEL
But he *has* to be there!

CANTWELL
(Into telephone)
Try his quarters, then. (*Softly, to himself*) Dammit, dammit, dammit.

MABEL
Are you sure General Conyers will back you up?

CANTWELL
He better. (*Into telephone*) Well, isn't there a phone anywhere near there? (*To* MABEL) He's playing golf! (*Into tele-*

125

phone) O.K. Tell him as soon as you find him to call Senator Cantwell, in Philadelphia. The number is Walnut 8-7593 . . . Got it? Thank you.

(CANTWELL *puts receiver down; he rises, starts to pace, thinking hard*)

MABEL

But you've *got* to talk to him before they come down here.

CANTWELL

It's too late now. (*Thoughtfully*) Maybe it's just as well . . . (*Starts to plan*) Now, let's see: Conyers . . . the delegates . . . Sheldon Marcus. (*Slowly*) Yes, Sheldon Marcus . . .

MABEL

Joe, I am scared to death . . .

CANTWELL

Well, don't be. (*Soothingly*) Come here, poor Momma Bear. (*He embraces her*) And don't worry. Poppa Bear isn't going to get shot down this close to the honey-tree.

MABEL

I just don't know how they can use something like that which is so untrue, which is a dirty lie and everybody knew it was a lie even at the time . . . Oh, how I hate politics!

(*The telephone rings.* CANTWELL *breaks away to answer it*)

CANTWELL

Conyers! (*Into telephone*) Yes? Who? (*Startled*) Oh, Mrs. Russell . . . Yes, this is Joe Cantwell . . . No, Bill isn't here yet. I guess he's still on his way down . . . *What?* Oh, that's awful! And you say he's . . . Yes, of course. Of course I'll tell Bill. The second he gets here. Yes. . . . He's a great guy. Yes, thank you. Good-by, Mrs. Russell. (*Puts down receiver*) Art Hockstader just collapsed. They've taken him to the hospital. He's dying.

MABEL

Dying? I thought he . . .

CANTWELL

That hernia stuff was a lot of bull.

MABEL

But what's this going to do to us, his dying now?

CANTWELL

Find out what hospital he's at.
(RUSSELL, BLADES *and* JENSEN *emerge from the bathroom into the bedroom.* CANTWELL *hears them. He gestures warningly to* MABEL, *who is about to exit right*)

CANTWELL

Not a word about Hockstader. I don't want anything to upset this meeting.
(MABEL *nods and goes.* CANTWELL *gets himself into position as the three men enter the living room*)

BLADES

Well, here we are!

JENSEN

Touch and go for a while there but we made it. Nobody saw us.

(RUSSELL *and* CANTWELL *stare at one another curiously.*
A long silence, interrupted by MABEL'S *return*)

MABEL
(*Gaily*)

Well, now, will you look at that! I tell you they look just like two wild animals in the zoo! (*Pause*) Well, come on now . . . somebody *say* something! It's just politics, that's all, isn't like the end of the world or anything . . .

JENSEN
(*Flatly*)

Yet.

MABEL

I had such a nice visit with your wife, Mr. Russell . . . and she is getting to be a real campaigner, isn't she? (*Starts to cross to bar*) Could I fix you a drink or something? We have just about everything. Let me see, there's gin and there's Scotch and there's bourbon with branch water like President Hockstader always used to . . .

(*She stops of her own accord, remembering*)

CANTWELL

I don't think we want a drink, Mabel.

RUSSELL

No, thank you.

MABEL
(*To* BLADES)

Well, in that case I believe we must make ourselves scarce, Don.

BLADES

(*To* RUSSELL)

Let me know when you're ready to go back upstairs.

(BLADES *exits right*)

CANTWELL

(*To* RUSSELL)

Is Sheldon Marcus in the hotel?

JENSEN

Yes.

CANTWELL

Could I see him? (*To* RUSSELL) I'd like to ask him some questions . . . in front of you, if it's all right.

(RUSSELL *nods*)

JENSEN

I'll bring him down.

CANTWELL

(*Indicates office to right*)

Have him wait in there.

(JENSEN *goes off stage, left*)

MABEL

Well, I guess you two boys want to be alone. (*To* RUSSELL) Now you go easy on my Joe . . . who is the best husband that ever was, ever! Well, good-by, now . . . (*To* CANTWELL, *nervously*) Joe honey, if you want me I'll be over in Sue-Ellen Gamadge's room, we're having a real old-time henfest this afternoon, with all the governors' wives . . .

(CANTWELL *nods to her, encouragingly.* MABEL *crosses through bedroom and exits left*)

CANTWELL

Well, Bill, here we are . . . the main event like they say.

RUSSELL

The main event. And here we stand, as Martin Luther said . . .

CANTWELL
(*Misunderstanding*)
Oh, I'm sorry . . . sit down, please . . .

RUSSELL

And it is not safe to move.

CANTWELL

Who said what?

RUSSELL

Martin Luther said: it is not safe to move. (*Explaining*) Luther was . . .

CANTWELL
(*Irritably*)
You don't need to tell me who Martin Luther was. I happen to be a Protestant. I'm a very religious kind of guy . . . Bill.

RUSSELL
(*Ironically*)
You don't need to tell *me* that . . . Joe.
(RUSSELL *sits on the sofa downstage.* CANTWELL *remains standing*)

CANTWELL
(*Stung*)

You really do think you're better than all of us, with your bad jokes, and the admiration of a lot of bleeding-heart fellow travelers and would-be intellectuals who don't mean a thing in this country!

RUSSELL
(*Appreciatively*)

That was very good, Joe. Pure Cantwell. Known as the multiple lie. Or in this case the multiple-lie-plus-confused-statement. For instance, you say that I think I'm better than the rest of you . . .

CANTWELL
(*Quickly*)

You don't deny . . .

RUSSELL
(*Chuckling*)

Excellent. Interrupt before the answer begins. That's vintage Cantwell . . .

CANTWELL
(*District Attorney's voice*)

I'm not interested in your sophistry. Your contempt. Your deliberate refusal to answer . . .

RUSSELL
(*Bangs ash tray on coffee table*)

Mr. Chairman! Mr. Chairman! Point of order! (*Laughs*) Oh, how're you going to keep them down in the Senate once they've been on TV?

CANTWELL
(*Smiles*)

Very funny. Very cute. I like that. You should have your own TV show.

RUSSELL

Thank you. I'm sure you meant that as a compliment. . . . Joe, I came down here to convince you that there are some things a man cannot do even in politics . . .
(CANTWELL *sits opposite him downstage*)

CANTWELL
(*Not listening*)

Now I have given you every hint, every opportunity in the past two days to pull out of the race. Considering your medical history, it could be done so easily . . . so logically. All you'd have to do is claim exhaustion, fatigue . . . like the last time . . . and then this ugly business would never come up and the Party could then unite behind its candidate . . .

RUSSELL

You?

CANTWELL
(*Nods*)

And we take the election in November.

RUSSELL

You make it sound so simple, but it isn't. For one thing, you'll be sued for the theft of my case history.

CANTWELL
(*Tries to interrupt*)

Bill . . .

132

RUSSELL

But that's not the point.

CANTWELL
(*Again*)

Bill . . .

RUSSELL

What I want you to realize . . .

CANTWELL
(*Voice of reason*)

Bill! I didn't steal it. The thing was *given* to me, unsolicited. Anyway, I'm sure your doctor won't file suit if you ask him not to.

RUSSELL
(*Taken aback*)

Why should I ask him not to?

CANTWELL
(*Promptly*)

Party unity. What's the point of smearing me when I'm the one who's got to get us into the White House?

RUSSELL

What makes you so certain *you're* going to be nominated?

CANTWELL
(*As to a child*)

Because I expect you to withdraw . . . because you've got no choice. Then who else is there? Except me.

RUSSELL

(*Stunned*)

You are . . . amazing! I came down here with enough political nitroglycerine not only to knock you out of the race but out of politics altogether, and there you sit and blandly tell me *I'm* the one to withdraw.

CANTWELL

(*Through him*)

I also promise to use you, once I'm elected. And that's a solemn promise, Bill. You can have any post in the cabinet you want, excepting Secretary of State, where I'm all hung up with somebody else. Or you can go as our first Ambassador to Red China . . . (RUSSELL *looks at him, amazed*) That's right. You'll be happy to know I intend to recognize Red China, though I won't make an issue of it until public opinion is more . . .

RUSSELL

(*Thoughtfully*)

Never defend, always attack. You're very good at this, Joe. I mean that.

CANTWELL

Another thing you ought to know since you've made such a point about it in your attacks on me: politically we are almost the same on every important issue. *Only* I am less reckless than you. I believe in timing. I don't see anything to be gained by launching a policy just to have it shot down maybe for good because the climate wasn't right.

RUSSELL

And you call that leadership?

CANTWELL

There are many ways of leading: the worst one is making brilliant speeches on the right side at the wrong time. I know how to wait . . .

RUSSELL

You are candid.

(CANTWELL, *bursting with energy and self-righteousness, starts to pace*)

CANTWELL

(*Passionately*)

And I'm right! Because I was born to this. You weren't. I know in my bones how to do this thing. I understand the people of this country. Because I'm one of them. I know how to maneuver. How to win. I knew from the time I won my first election I was going to be President and nobody was going to stop me. Not even the brilliant, witty, aristocratic, intellectual William Russell, who has no more to do with the people of this country than I have to do with the Groton Harvard Wall Street set.

RUSSELL

Well, there is no immediate need to start a class war. I am not better qualified to be President because I went to Harvard than you are because you worked your way through a state college. But as you probably know there is a certain suspicion of the self-made man these days. People aren't as naïve as you think. Any man who fights his way to the top is certainly to be admired, but the people sometimes wonder: how exactly did he do it? And whom did he hurt along the way? The self-made man often makes himself out of pieces of his victims. (RUSSELL *rises and crosses to* CANTWELL *as his own rage begins*) You are something of a Frankenstein monster, Joe, made out of the bits and pieces of

Sicilian bandits . . . and your political opponents . . . all assembled before our eyes on television.

CANTWELL
(*Coldly*)
How I was made is not the question. What matters is, I am here.

RUSSELL
And you think that your basic public *image* has changed?

CANTWELL
It has. According to the Gallup poll only twelve per cent of the people even remember that there was a Mafia hearing.

RUSSELL
I remember.

CANTWELL
The image that they have of Cantwell is the way I am now . . .

RUSSELL
Smooth, cautious, beyond reproach . . .

CANTWELL
That is right. People forget. Nobody's going to get any mileage out of my past so let's get this Aleutian business over with. I'm going to question Sheldon Marcus now and you're going to get the surprise of your life.
(RUSSELL *turns away from him; he sits again on the sofa*)

RUSSELL
Nothing *you* do ever surprises me, Joe. What *I* do, however, is

beginning to surprise me. (*He touches the folder in his jacket pocket*) I never thought I could bring up something like this against any man. It revolts me . . .

CANTWELL
(*Generously*)

Oh, come on! Don't give it a second thought. Look, I don't blame you. I'd certainly use it against you if it was there . . .

RUSSELL

That's the point; *you* would. I wouldn't. Or never thought I would.

(CANTWELL *sees a possible break in the enemy line*)

CANTWELL

Then what are you doing down here? What have you got this joker Marcus standing by for except to smear me as a homosexual which I'm not.

RUSSELL

I never said you were . . .

CANTWELL
(*Relentlessly*)

Then what are you doing here if you don't think I am?

RUSSELL

Had you paused at any point in your offensive, I would have told you *why* I came here and *what* I mean to do.

CANTWELL
(*Triumphantly*)

I hope you realize you have just admitted that you don't believe this accusation against me. That you are openly confessing collusion . . .

CENTER

RUSSELL
(*Abruptly*)

Joe, shut up! (*Rises*) Art Hockstader was right when he said you're not very sensitive to people. You're so busy trying to win you never stop to figure out *what* it is you're winning.

CANTWELL
(*Simulated weariness*)

I am only trying to stick to the issue at hand. I don't believe in indulging in personalities.

RUSSELL

Come off it, Joe! I came here to try and convince you to drop that nonsense against me just as I mean to drop this nonsense against you. These things are irrelevant and dishonest, not to mention untrue. They cancel each other out. So I wish you would please join me by *not* indulging in personalities. (*Holds up folder*) I'll tear this up and send Sheldon Marcus back where he came from, if you drop that business against me.

CANTWELL
(*Nods*)

I see. You came here to make a deal with me.

RUSSELL
(*A sigh of exasperation*)

No! I came here to . . .
(CANTWELL *is growing confident*)

138

CANTWELL

(*Warmly*)

Look, Bill, it makes perfect sense, what you're doing. And I have no hard feelings. Really, I mean it. (CANTWELL *pats* RUSSELL *on the back*) So don't be apologetic.

RUSSELL

You have *no* feelings, I would say.

CANTWELL

And perhaps you have too many. Perhaps you *are* too emotional. The report on your breakdown said you might have thought of committing suicide . . .

RUSSELL

Who hasn't thought of it?

CANTWELL

I never have. And I don't think a President should. No matter how tough the going is.

RUSSELL

(*Amused*)

Am I to understand you want to save the country from me? That you are genuinely afraid I'm unstable?

CANTWELL

Yes, I am. You just admitted you thought of suicide . . .

RUSSELL

Then, Joe, if I'm so unstable, why did you offer me the ambassadorship to Red China?

CANTWELL

(*Promptly*)

The President can keep tabs on an ambassador. Nobody can keep tabs on a President.

RUSSELL

(*Nods*)

Never pause for an answer, in the best tradition of a television performer. . . . Well, let's get this dirty business over with. I won't throw my mud if you won't throw your mud.

CANTWELL

And we go into convention tomorrow and you get nominated on the first ballot? No.

RUSSELL

Well, then . . . good luck. And may "the best man" win, assuming we don't knock each other off *and* the Party.

(RUSSELL *turns to go.* CANTWELL *signals frantically*)

CANTWELL

Now wait a minute . . . Wait a minute! Bill! I realize we've got to work something out. And I'm willing to be reasonable, only you have *got* to . . .

RUSSELL

(*Exploding*)

Stop it! Either we declare a moratorium on mud or we both let fly.

(*Swiftly* CANTWELL *shifts his tack. He goes to door at right*)

CANTWELL

O.K. (*Opens door, looks through into office*) Don, send Mr.

Marcus in. (*To* RUSSELL) Can I see that court-martial testimony? (RUSSELL *gives him testimony. He studies it, as* MARCUS *enters, nervously. A long moment. Then* CANTWELL *speaks, still studying documents*) Hi, Shelly, how's the boy? Long time no see.

MARCUS

Yeah . . . Joe . . . long time. . . . Hello again, Mr. Russell.

RUSSELL

Joe wants to ask you some questions . . .

MARCUS

Well, I really ought to be getting back to Wilmington, you see, my wife . . .

CANTWELL

You live in Wilmington, eh? Great town . . . used to have some cousins there named Everly, Jack and Helen Everly, maybe you know them, in real estate . . .

MARCUS

Well, it's not Wilmington proper, actually, where I live, it's a suburb where Peggy and I live. I don't think I know anybody named (*For the first time* CANTWELL *looks at* MARCUS, *who steps back in alarm*) Everly . . .

CANTWELL
(*Smiles*)

Shelly, you put on a lot of weight.

MARCUS

Well, it's Peggy . . . it's my wife Peggy's cooking, she's a

141

wonderful cook . . . (*Close to tears*) I thought, Mr. Russell, I wouldn't have to . . . to . . .

CANTWELL

To see your old buddy? Now you know I would've been fit to be tied if I had known Shelly Marcus from Adak was in town and hadn't come to see me.

MARCUS

Well, I . . . I know how busy you are . . . *both* you men are . . . running for this President thing, and I was just . . . well, passing by.

CANTWELL
(*Pleasantly*)

And you thought you would pause just long enough to smear your old buddy?

MARCUS

Now, Joe, don't get mad at me . . . it was . . . it was my duty!

CANTWELL

To get even with me for seeing you were passed over for promotion because of incompetence. (*To* RUSSELL) Always a good idea to start with the motive.

RUSSELL
(*To* MARCUS)

Is this true?

MARCUS
(*Taken aback*)

Well, no, not really . . . I mean my efficiency report was . . .

CANTWELL

(*In for the death*)

Can be found in army records! Unsatisfactory! I was adjutant and I personally stopped his promotion *and* his transfer *and* he knew it. (*Picks up documents*) Now, on 6 April 1944 into my quonset hut at the army base on Adak there moved a Lieutenant Fenn . . .

MARCUS

That was the one, like I told you . . . that was the one . . . we all knew . . .

CANTWELL

We shared the same hut for three months.

MARCUS

Just the two of them. Like I told you. It's all in the record there . . . they were, you know . . . they were . . .

CANTWELL

(*Inexorably*)

Fenn was caught with an enlisted man *in flagrante delicto* on the afternoon of 14 June 1944 in the back of the post church. The M.P.s caught him . . .

MARCUS

(*Rapidly*)

That's right. And that's when he broke down and told about everything and everybody . . . the M.P.s laid this trap for him . . . they'd been tipped off . . .

CANTWELL

By the Advocate General . . .

MARCUS

That's right. By Colonel Conyers, he was the one finally broke up this whole ring of degenerates . . . And Fenn when he was caught gave, oh, maybe twenty, thirty names and one of those names was Joe Cantwell, his roommate . . .

CANTWELL

Correct. Now: what happened to those twenty-eight officers and men who were named at the court-martial?

MARCUS

They were all separated from the service . . . Section 8 we called it . . . for the good of the service, they were all kicked out . . .

CANTWELL

All except one.

MARCUS

That's right . . . all except you.

CANTWELL

(*Smiles at* RUSSELL)

And why wasn't I?

MARCUS

I . . . well . . . I don't know. I suppose it's in the records or something. But I know I thought then what a lot of people thought: how Joe must've pulled some pretty fancy wires to save his neck. Yes, sir, he was a real operator, he could get out of *anything*, and that's the truth . . . Anyways, it's all there in the court-martial; how he was one of them, named under oath by Lieutenant Fenn.

RUSSELL
(*To* MARCUS)

Where is Lieutenant Fenn now?

CANTWELL

He's dead.

MARCUS

That's right, he died after the war in that plane crash, you remember the one? Out in Detroit, that freak one where the light-
ning hit the engine and . . .

RUSSELL
(*To* CANTWELL)

If you were innocent, why did Fenn name you?

CANTWELL
(*Coldly, carefully*)

Because I was the one who turned him in.

MARCUS
(*Stunned*)

You were!

CANTWELL

This clown wouldn't know but I'm ashamed of *you*, Bill, for not
doing your homework, for not checking with a certain Colonel,
now Major General, Conyers who was the Advocate General up
there. (*Turns on* MARCUS, *who retreats before him*) You see,
Shelly, when I found out what was going on I went to Conyers
and told him what I had discovered about my roommate. We
laid a trap for Fenn and he fell into it. At the trial I gave secret
evidence against him and that's why he named me: *in revenge*,

145

and that's why no action was ever or could ever be taken against me. (*To* RUSSELL) I even got promoted on the strength of having helped clear those types out of our command.

MARCUS

Oh, I bet that isn't so . . . I bet you'll find he sneaked out of it like he did everything else . . . I know Joe Cantwell . . .

RUSSELL
(*To* CANTWELL)

Can you prove this?
(CANTWELL *nods. He is now upstage at desk*)

CANTWELL

A few minutes ago I talked with the Advocate General. His name is Conyers. He's in Colorado now. He told me he would back me up. In every way. (CANTWELL *gives* RUSSELL *the telephone number*) Here's his name and phone number. He's expecting a call from you, Bill. (*Like a carnivore*, CANTWELL *stalks the terrified* MARCUS *to the door*) And now, Shelly Marcus, if you ever say one word about this to anybody, I will have you up for libel, *criminal* libel . . .

MARCUS

Now, look here, Joe, don't you threaten me . . .
(MARCUS *grabs his briefcase and raincoat and tries to get to the corridor door before* CANTWELL *reaches him*)

CANTWELL

In fact, I will involve you personally in that whole mess at Adak and by the time I finish with you . . .

MARCUS

Don't you bully me, Joe, don't you try to intimidate me . . .

CANTWELL

I'll make you wish you'd never been born!

(*Just as* CANTWELL *seems about to seize him,* MARCUS *bolts into the connecting hall. He opens the corridor door. But to his horror,* NEWSMEN *and* PHOTOGRAPHERS *burst in. He is borne straight back to* CANTWELL, *who smiles and straightens* MARCUS's *jacket. Then he turns him about for the* PHOTOGRAPHERS, *who want a picture*)

CANTWELL

Just one second . . . (*Puts arm about* MARCUS's *shoulders*) Sure was swell to see you, Shelly. Next time when you drop by, bring the wife, bring . . . uh, Peggy. Mabel and I'd love to meet her. Love to see you both. You come see us now in Washington. (*Poses again with* MARCUS) How's that?

PHOTOGRAPHER

Hold it!

(MARCUS *goes, surrounded by* NEWSMEN. CANTWELL *shuts the corridor door after them. He pauses a moment in the connecting hall, unobserved by* RUSSELL. *He passes his hand wearily across his face. Then he pulls himself together and returns to the living room*)

CANTWELL

I'm sorry to disappoint you, Bill, but this won't work. I'm covered on every side. You won't be able to make this thing stick for two minutes. And I should also warn you: this is the kind of desperate last-minute smear that always backfires on the guy who makes it. Ask Art Hockstader. He'll tell you. (RUSSELL *stares at*

147

him with a fascinated revulsion) Well, go on. If you don't believe me, you got General Conyers' number in your hand. Call him.

RUSSELL

True? False? We've both gone beyond the "truth" now. We're in dangerous country.
(RUSSELL *drops the paper with the telephone number on the sofa*)

CANTWELL
(*Begins*)
Every word I said was true . . .

RUSSELL

You are worse than a liar. You have no sense of right or wrong. Only what will work. (RUSSELL *picks up court-martial testimony*) Well, *this* is going to work.

CANTWELL

But you're not going to use that now!

RUSSELL

Oh, yes! Yes! I'll use *anything* against you. I can't let you be President.
(RUSSELL *crosses to bedroom.* CANTWELL *tries to block his way.* RUSSELL *pushes him aside. Both men go into bedroom*)

CANTWELL

Hey! What are you going to do? Bill, you're not really going to use that stuff. You can't. Look, it's . . . it's too dirty! Honest to God, nobody will believe it! (RUSSELL *pauses at the bathroom door. He looks at* CANTWELL; *then he turns and goes into the bath-*

room. CANTWELL, *near breaking, shouts after him*) O.K. Russell, go ahead, it's your funeral. Against me, you haven't got a chance. (CANTWELL *sits down on the bed, his back to the audience. For the first time he seems exhausted, played out. Then he picks up the bedside telephone*) Send Don Blades in . . . and keep trying on that Colorado call.

(BLADES *enters living room from right. He hurries into bedroom.* CANTWELL *does not acknowledge him*)

BLADES

Well, what happened? (BLADES *peers into bathroom*) Where's Russell? Joe? (*Sudden alarm*) Hey, Joe!

(CANTWELL *is recalled from some private reverie. He looks at* BLADES; *he smiles suddenly; his tone is casual*)

CANTWELL

Oh, Don, hi.

(CANTWELL *rises and crosses to living room.* BLADES *follows*)

BLADES

What's Russell up to? What's this all about? What's he got on you?

CANTWELL

(*Thoughtfully*)

You know what that guy said just now? He said I wasn't very sensitive about other people. He said I didn't understand character . . .

BLADES

Is that what he came down here for? To give you a lecture?

CANTWELL

(*Nods*)

Yeah. Pretty much. (CANTWELL *sees the paper with* GENERAL CONYERS' *telephone number on it; he picks it up; he smiles*) Well, I have news for him. I am a very good judge of character. (*Abruptly*) You can release that stuff on Russell now. One copy to every delegate. (*Excitement*) Don, we're home free. (*He rolls the paper into a tight wad*) And I'll make you a bet: Russell quits before the first ballot. (CANTWELL *flicks the wad across the room. The room goes dark*)

CURTAIN

ACT THREE

Scene Two

Russell suite. The next afternoon. The television set is on.
JENSEN *watches it while going through papers at the desk.*
There is band music from the convention hall. In the bed-
room, ALICE *finishes packing. The telephone rings.*

JENSEN
(Answers it)
Who? Oh, Senator Joseph. No, he's not back yet. No, I don't
know what to do. He's still over at the hospital. He's with President Hockstader and there's no way to phone . . . I guess we
just stand by. How's the balloting? *(Frowns)* Oh, no!
  *(*RUSSELL *enters from corridor, murmuring "No comment"*
to the press)

JENSEN
Wait a minute, Senator. He's here. *(To* RUSSELL*)* Bill, it's Senator Joseph. He's in the convention hall. They're into the sixth
ballot. It's still a deadlock. Cantwell's leading but nobody's got a
majority. Merwin's sitting tight. Joseph says if you let him blast
Cantwell now, we're in on the next ballot.

RUSSELL
What was the voting on the fifth ballot?

151

JENSEN

(*Looks at paper*)

Cantwell 474, Russell 386, Merwin 214 . . . all the favorite sons are gone. And nobody's budging yet.

RUSSELL

What about Merwin? If I were to get his 214 votes . . .

JENSEN

You'd win. But he's hanging on. Senator Joseph's trying to reach him now, to see if he'll take on second spot with you . . .

RUSSELL

Cantwell must be trying the same thing . . .

JENSEN

Merwin's holding out for the best possible terms.

RUSSELL

(*Smiles*)

He's showing unexpected character, isn't he?

JENSEN

(*Urgently*)

You've *got* to make up your mind! You've got to let our boys get that stuff on Cantwell to the delegates. We can ask for a recess before the seventh ballot. Then . . .

RUSSELL

Tell the Senator to wait.

JENSEN

But we *can't* wait . . .

RUSSELL
(*Firmly*)

I said, wait, Dick.

JENSEN
(*Into telephone*)

Not yet . . . (*He hangs up*) Bill, what's wrong with you? We've lost a night and a day, but one word from you and we can still wreck Joe Cantwell.

RUSSELL

I know.

JENSEN

Then why are you holding back? What have you got to lose? Joe's done his worst. Every delegation's got a copy of your case history and believe it or not we're still in business. I don't know why, but we are.

RUSSELL

Which means perhaps that dirt does not always stick . . .

JENSEN

Enough did. You lost three hundred votes because of it.

RUSSELL

But not all to Cantwell. Merwin picked up over a hundred of my votes. And that is a sign of something . . .

JENSEN

Disgust.

RUSSELL

Or human decency.

JENSEN

Decency? At a *convention?*

RUSSELL

(*Smiles*)

I am an optimist.

(RUSSELL *goes into the bedroom*)

ALICE

I packed. I thought no matter what happens, we'll be leaving tonight.

RUSSELL

Yes, we'll be leaving.

ALICE

How was Art?

RUSSELL

They wouldn't let me see him today. He's still unconscious.

(JENSEN, *who has been watching the television set, leaps to his feet and goes to the bedroom*)

JENSEN

(*Desperately*)

Bill, I don't want to press you, but will you please make up your mind. The sixth ballot's almost over and . . . (*Telephone in bedroom rings;* JENSEN *answers it*) Who? Oh, it's you . . . He does? Now? (*To* RUSSELL) It's Don Blades. Cantwell wants to see you.

RUSSELL

I'm sure he does. (*Smiles*) All right. Tell him to come up. I'd like to see Joe again.

(RUSSELL *goes into living room;* ALICE *follows*)

JENSEN
(*Into telephone*)
O.K. He'll see you. (*Puts receiver down*)

ALICE
(*To* RUSSELL)
What do you think Cantwell wants?

RUSSELL
A deal. What else does Joe Cantwell ever want. (*Picks up newspaper*) Oh, have you seen his latest statement? "The rumors about William Russell's health have been maliciously exaggerated." He's wonderful!

JENSEN
Look, before he gets here, let me call Senator Joseph . . .

RUSSELL
No, Dick.

JENSEN
But yesterday you were willing to do anything!

RUSSELL
That was yesterday. I lost my temper. And did rather a poor imitation of Joe Cantwell. I was remarkably melodramatic. I even turned my own stomach. But today I'm myself again!

JENSEN
Bill . . .

ALICE
Leave him alone, Dick.

155

RUSSELL

There is a certain relief to knowing that the worst has happened to you and you're still alive . . . and kicking. (*Looks at television set*) Ah . . . there's my old friend Senator Carlin. True to the end.

(RUSSELL *turns up volume*)

CARLIN'S VOICE
(*Booming*)

. . . This Sovereign State casts forty-four votes for the next Preznighstays Joe Cantwell!

(RUSSELL *turns the volume off*)

RUSSELL
(*Thoughtfully*)

Senator Carlin has every characteristic of a dog, except loyalty.

(BLADES *and* CANTWELL *enter. The press is violent in its attentions. With some difficulty, they are got out of the room*)

BLADES

Gentlemen . . .

CANTWELL

Hello, Bill . . .

RUSSELL
(*Gaily*)

Hi, Joe! What a nice surprise, your coming here like this!

CANTWELL

Yes. . . . Mrs. Russell, I'm Joe Cantwell . . . I don't think we've met. (CANTWELL *shakes* ALICE's *hand*)

ALICE

How do you do.

CANTWELL
(*Mechanically*)
We talked on the phone, I guess.

RUSSELL

Sit down, Joe. (CANTWELL *sits*) I thought you would be busy working on your acceptance speech. Or is it already written?

CANTWELL
(*Begins*)
Now, Bill, as I see the picture . . .

RUSSELL

I've been working for months on *my* acceptance speech, trying to strike that delicate balance between humility and confidence.

CANTWELL

Yes. Now as I see this convention . . .

RUSSELL

You of course have a gift for hitting the right note.

CANTWELL

Yes . . .

RUSSELL

I like the way you always manage to state the obvious with u sense of real discovery.

CANTWELL

Yes. Now, Bill . . .

RUSSELL

And that wonderful trick you have for . . .

CANTWELL

(*Exploding*)

Bill, at least let me get one word in edgewise!

RUSSELL

(*Laughs*)

I'm sorry, Joe. I couldn't resist it. (*To the others*) I was using Joe's technique: never let the other man get started. Talk right through him. Also, whenever Joe starts a sentence with "Now, Bill" . . . you know he's up to no good.

CANTWELL

(*Quickly*)

Now, Bill . . .

RUSSELL

See?

(CANTWELL *controls himself with some difficulty*)

CANTWELL

Very cute. Bill, this convention is really hung up and the way things are going we may never nominate anybody.

BLADES

And who wants to spend the next four years in Philadelphia?

CANTWELL

Believe me when I say I have given the whole thing a lot of thought: and I want you to be on my ticket.

RUSSELL

Well, that's very generous, Joe. But tell me, how can I possibly run for Vice-President when I am at this very moment suffering from one of my frequent nervous breakdowns?

CANTWELL

There was no way of keeping a report like that secret. Anyway, you've got to admit we handled the whole thing darned well. I mean look at the papers: practically no mention . . .

RUSSELL

Just as there was no mention of the fact that Art Hockstader is dying?

CANTWELL

Art didn't want anybody to know how sick he was. Did he, Mrs. Russell? He was a great old guy. You know he's dead, don't you? (RUSSELL *rises, shaken.* CANTWELL *does not notice the other man's response*) Now, as I see the picture, delegate-wise . . .

RUSSELL

I didn't know . . . Art was dead.

CANTWELL

Oh? Yeah, he died about half an hour ago. He knew it was all over last night when I saw him.

RUSSELL
(*Startled*)

You saw him?

CANTWELL

That's right. Just for a few minutes, while he was still conscious . . .

RUSSELL

Oh, no, no! Don't tell us that Art Hockstader with his dying breath said, "Bless you, Joe, go to it!" And handed on the torch.

(CANTWELL *gets to his feet, angrily*)

CANTWELL

You certainly like to jump to conclusions, don't you? If you really want to know what Art said, I'll tell you: he said, "To hell with both of you," meaning you as well as me.

BLADES

He sure was a funny old bird. Full of hell right to the end. But his day was done . . . just as well he conked out when he did.

(ALICE *goes into the bedroom*)

RUSSELL

Will you two please get out?

JENSEN

Bill!

(RUSSELL *turns to follow* ALICE)

CANTWELL

Look, Russell, for a lot of reasons we want you on the ticket and, frankly, if I were you, I'd show a little . . . well, gratitude.

(RUSSELL *wheels about, fiercely*)

RUSSELL

Gratitude! Do you realize all I have to do is call Senator Joseph . . .

BLADES

(*Quickly*)

But you know that story about Joe was a bum rap, so how could you use it?

RUSSELL

Since when has the truth been a deterrent at this convention? It is also not true that I am mentally unstable . . .

BLADES

(*Quickly*)

But it *is* true that you had a mental breakdown, and that is a fact the voters should know.

(CANTWELL *stops* BLADES *with a gesture*)

CANTWELL

Bill, I solemnly promise before these witnesses that I will give you anything you want . . . the Vice-Presidency, Secretary of State . . . commitment or no commitment . . . it's yours if you throw me your votes on the next ballot.

JENSEN

(*Delighted*)

Bill, come on, they're scared!

BLADES

Oh, no, we're not!

JENSEN

They're sweating ice!

CANTWELL

I want a united front, for the sake of the Party.

JENSEN

Look at them squirm!

BLADES

Who's squirming? Anyway, we got all the votes we need right now.

JENSEN

Where?

BLADES

Governor Merwin.

JENSEN

He won't play with you.

BLADES

He's offered to. But Joe doesn't want Merwin on the ticket. He'd rather have the Secretary here . . .

JENSEN

Merwin refused to be on the ticket with Joe and you know it . . . if he'd agreed, you wouldn't be up here, sweating!

BLADES
(Angrily)

I am not sweating!

JENSEN

Bill, we've got them. We've really got them. Let me call Senator Joseph?

CANTWELL

I wish you would. And tell him you'll support me, in the interest of Party unity, and that you'll accept the second spot on the ticket . . .

JENSEN
(Overlaps)

And tell him you're ready to lower the boom on Cantwell?
(RUSSELL *at bedroom door. He looks at* ALICE. *He decides*)

RUSSELL

All right, call him.

(ALICE *returns to the living room. She sits on the down-stage sofa*)

JENSEN

Put me through to Senator Joseph. Extension 12, convention hall . . . Hello . . . that you, Senator? Well, brace yourself. This is it. Our man is about to fight . . .

(RUSSELL *comes to telephone*)

BLADES

(*Pleads*)

Russell, don't. You *can't* use that stuff. Joe's our only hope. He's the Party's only hope.

CANTWELL

Shut up, Don. We don't have to worry about Mr. Russell. He always does the right thing.

RUSSELL

(*To* CANTWELL)

Thank you. (*Into telephone*) Senator? This is William Russell. I'm coming down to the convention hall in a few minutes to make a statement. Before I do, I want you to get to the chairman of the next delegation pledged to me . . . Utah? All right. Tell the chairman to announce to the convention that I have withdrawn from the race.

JENSEN

(*Aghast*)

Bill!

BLADES
(*Ecstatic*)
Mr. Secretary, I swear you won't regret . . .

RUSSELL
And that I am releasing my 384 delegates with instructions to support Governor John Merwin.

JENSEN
Merwin!

BLADES
But . . . but you can't . . .
(RUSSELL *puts the receiver down*)

RUSSELL
I can. And I have.

JENSEN
Merwin's nobody!

RUSSELL
Well, he is now somebody . . . (*Turns to* CANTWELL, *who has sunk to a bench, his hand over his face*) Neither the angel of darkness nor the angel of light . . . if I may exaggerate my goodness . . . has carried the day. We canceled each other out.
(JENSEN *indicates the television set*)

JENSEN
(*Bitterly*)
Allowing the angel of grayness to win, as usual.

164

RUSSELL

The light blinds us . . . and we're all afraid of the dark. (*To* CANTWELL) I meant it, Joe, when I said I could never let you be President.

BLADES
(*Viciously*)
Well, you just cut your own throat. You are through in politics.

RUSSELL

Joe Cantwell is through in politics.
(BLADES *crosses to upstage door*)

BLADES

He had a deal! I bet he had a deal with Merwin all along, the tricky son of a . . .
(BLADES *slams the door after him.* CANTWELL *looks at* RUSSELL *for the first time; he is genuinely puzzled*)

CANTWELL
(*Slowly*)
I don't understand you.

RUSSELL

I know you don't. Because you have no sense of responsibility toward anybody or anything and that is a tragedy in a man and it is a disaster in a President! You said you were religious. Well, I'm not. But I believe profoundly in *this* life and what we do to one another and how this monstrous "I," the self, must become "we" and draw the line at murder in the games we play with one another, and try to be good even when there is no one to force us to be good.
(CANTWELL *rises. He speaks carefully, without rancor*)

165

CANTWELL

You don't understand me. You don't understand politics. You don't understand this country and the way it is and the way we are. You are a fool.

(CANTWELL *goes, shutting the corridor door after him.* RUSSELL *shakes his head*)

RUSSELL

We're not the way Joe thinks we are. At least not yet.

JENSEN

You don't even know Merwin. Nobody knows him. He's a man without a face.

RUSSELL

Don't underestimate him. Men without faces tend to get elected President, and power or responsibility or honor fill in the features, usually pretty well.

JENSEN

I'm afraid, Bill, your conscience is my enemy.

(JENSEN *goes off stage right.* RUSSELL *looks after him a moment, then he notices the "Hustle with Russell" placard*)

RUSSELL

(*Smiles*)

Well, everyone hustled except Russell. (*Notices television set*) Here comes Utah.

(RUSSELL *turns up volume*)

DELEGATE'S VOICE

State of Utah at the instruction of that great American and Secretary of State William Russell (*Cheering*) casts its fourteen pledged votes to the next Preznighstays that great Governor John Merwin!

COMMENTATOR'S VOICE

This is the break in the deadlock! An unexpected development! There's real excitement down on the floor . . .

(RUSSELL *turns off set*)

RUSSELL

There it is! (*To* ALICE) Well, we've got work to do. Do you want to come down to the convention? Or wait here till I get back?

ALICE

I'll go with you.

RUSSELL

What . . . do you think?

ALICE

I wish you'd been nominated.

RUSSELL

So do I.

ALICE

But I like the way you . . . really won.

RUSSELL

Thank you. Life is a choice, they say. I've made mine.

ALICE

(*Smiles*)

And without doing your one-two-three walk.

167

RUSSELL

You know, Alice, you don't have to stay with me, if you don't want to.

ALICE

I know I don't have to.

RUSSELL
(*Tentatively*)

But . . . *would* you like to? Even though you'll never have the chance to be another Grace Coolidge?

ALICE

Now it's *my* turn to choose? (RUSSELL *nods*) Of course I'll stay.

(ALICE *rises*)

RUSSELL

I'm glad. But I warn you: the fires of autumn burn notoriously low.

ALICE
(*Smiles*)

Well, I've been cold such a long time.

(RUSSELL *takes her arm. They start to go upstage to the corridor door when* REPORTERS *burst in from stage right. Ad-libbed cries of "Statement!" Flash-bulbs go off.* RUSSELL *finally quiets them*)

RUSSELL

You may say that I think Governor Merwin will make a fine candidate, and I shall do everything I can to help him and the Party. (*Starts to go, pauses*) Oh. (*Smiles*) And I am of course happy: the best man won!

(RUSSELL *and* ALICE *followed by* REPORTERS *cross upstage, as the* CURTAIN FALLS)